"This is a fresh approach and much-needed resource for today's parents. An essential book for those who wish to instill 'non-tech' problem-solving skills for real world problems that children face in the 21st century. Powell's personal stories and powerful insight combine to make this an easy read. The book is filled with helpful strategies and the questions at the end of each chapter are a great learning tool and resource. Truly, this is a book that is ideal for those working with children suffering from trauma."

—*Dr. John DeGarmo, leading expert in foster care and parenting, founder of The Foster Care Institute*

"This book gives fun ways to engage children in physical as well as mental activities during difficult times of pain or hurt. The physical activities especially strengthen muscle memory, providing a vast opportunity for children who will benefit from this well-written and timely book!"

—*Dawn D'Amico, LCSW, PhD, author of* 101 Mindful Arts-Based Activities to Get Children and Adolescents Talking

"What I find most interesting about Beth Powell's work is the connections she makes between the physical, the neurological, and the emotional. She reminds us that physical play and creative play are vital for healthy human growth and must retain significance in this world of electronic and passive stimulants."

—*Dr. Brandy Harvey, Dean of Instruction, Lone Star College, Montgomery*

"*Fun Games and Physical Activities to Help Heal Children Who Hurt* is unlike anything I've yet to read! Ms. Powell breaks the typical activity book barrier with a masterpiece much more personal. This book is what this generation needs: let's replace the tech and retrain the brain. A great read for parents, teachers, and people seeking out tools to reach the neglected and traumatized."

—*Troy Skeen, former director and founder of a nationally recognized treatment facility for traumatized children*

D0145498

Fun Games and Physical Activities to Help Heal Children Who Hurt

of related interest

**101 Mindful Arts-Based Activities to Get
Children and Adolescents Talking**
Working with Severe Trauma, Abuse and Neglect
Using Found and Everyday Objects
Dawn D'Amico, LCSW, PhD
ISBN 978 1 78592 731 7
eISBN 978 1 78450 422 9

**A Therapeutic Treasure Box for Working with Children
and Adolescents with Developmental Trauma**
Creative Techniques and Activities
Dr. Karen Treisman
ISBN 978 1 78592 263 3
eISBN 978 1 78450 553 0

More Creative Coping Skills for Children
Activities, Games, Stories, and Handouts to Help Children Self-regulate
Bonnie Thomas
ISBN 978 1 78592 021 9
eISBN 978 1 78450 267 6

Fun Games and Physical Activities to Help Heal Children Who Hurt

GET ON YOUR FEET!

BETH POWELL, LCSW

Jessica Kingsley *Publishers*
London and Philadelphia

With kind thanks to Dr. Roger Leslie and Juanita Stanley for their help with editing.

First published in 2018
by Jessica Kingsley Publishers
73 Collier Street
London N1 9BE, UK
and
400 Market Street, Suite 400
Philadelphia, PA 19106, USA

www.jkp.com

Copyright © Beth Powell 2018

Front cover image source: Shutterstock®.

All rights reserved. No part of this publication may be reproduced in any material form (including photocopying, storing in any medium by electronic means or transmitting) without the written permission of the copyright owner except in accordance with the provisions of the law or under terms of a licence issued in the UK by the Copyright Licensing Agency Ltd. www.cla.co.uk or in overseas territories by the relevant reproduction rights organisation, for details see www.ifrro.org. Applications for the copyright owner's written permission to reproduce any part of this publication should be addressed to the publisher.

Warning: The doing of an unauthorised act in relation to a copyright work may result in both a civil claim for damages and criminal prosecution.

Library of Congress Cataloging in Publication Data
A CIP catalog record for this book is available from the Library of Congress

British Library Cataloguing in Publication Data
A CIP catalogue record for this book is available from the British Library

ISBN 978 1 78592 773 7
eISBN 978 1 78450 678 0

Printed and bound in the United States

Contents

Acknowledgments

Thank you, thank you, to editors Dr. Roger Leslie and Juanita Stanley. I may not be the best writer in the world, but I can sure talk. Bless you for your writing and editing skills and for helping me transfer what I had to say onto the written page.

Thank you, Bill Boyd, Graphics Artist, for the hours you worked taking photos, designing charts, making other visuals and formatting clip art to illustrate what I saw in my head and needed the reader to see with me.

Thank you, Donetta Ingling and siblings David and Lizbeth Lopez for playing games with me and posing for pictures of the fun we were having. Your natural inner joy shines through your faces and onto the pages of this book. Thank you for the blessing.

Thank you, unnamed parents who allowed me to use stories of your "hurting" children. Your stories will help so many other caregivers help their children heal.

Judith Bluestone, I wish you were still here as you had so much more to teach me and others. I am so grateful I learned from you what I did when you were here with us in physical form. I pray you are pleased with how I integrated the knowledge you gave me into work with traumatized children. I'll see you in Heaven.

And thank you, Grandmother Powell, Aunt Vernon, and Miss Beetles. What would I have done without the three of you when I was growing up? Thank you for being there for me and understanding what I needed when I was a child. You believed in me; I could feel it. And I return that love. I'll see you again one day, too!

And lastly, thank you Jessica Kingsley Publishers for liking my proposal and publishing this book! Sarah Hamlin, you are wonderful to work with.

Introduction

This book, subtitled *Get On Your Feet!*, provides caregivers of neglected/abused/traumatized children with information and guidance for using "no-tech" activities that develop children's brains and strengthen their ability and willingness to trust and attach to trustworthy others. These activities help children emotionally and neurologically traumatized by neglect and abuse in the early stages of life, including the in utero period. This book also helps caregivers understand the sources of their children's symptoms and offers the rationale for why all children should be moving and playing in "no-tech" creative, neuro-behavioral ways. Through "no-tech" interactive relationships and creative neuro-behavioral play, children's brains and bonds do grow.

The text contains many traditional games and activities that the author enjoyed growing up in the American Deep South before toys required batteries and microchips. Such "real world" experiences prompted face-to-face interactions with other human beings that made play therapeutic and human interaction fun and socio-emotionally stimulating.

The book enhances the activities with explanations for how and why specific creative play themes, games, and caregiver attitudes can help children's brains and bonds develop in ways that two-dimensional surfaces such as televisions, computers, and electronic hand-held devices cannot. It also explains how children learn to problem solve real-life situations by playing them out repeatedly to find hope, courage, and resiliency. Further benefits include how the practice of certain physical body movements and exercise can improve lower, more basic brain functions that support the higher thinking and problem-solving areas of the brain.

This book draws from both the author's professional experience in the field and her personal triumphs over both in utero and post-utero stress from a birth mother who suffered from mental illness and drank while pregnant with her. Beyond effective, hands-on, traditional activities, and stories with a spiritual twist, it offers a unique, personal perspective from an overcomer who has gone on to live and share the positive results of "no-tech" play.

Further, the author shares stories of "hurting children," including herself, so that readers can better understand not only what these children go through, but also what is needed to help them do more than survive, to thrive. These stories may remind readers of children they know and care for. More profoundly, they may help readers better understand why the children behave as they do and learn better ways to help them.

This book is divided into two sections. The first offers basic background information about how early trauma impacts children's brains and relationships, and how caregivers can set the stage for recovery and growth by the structure of their caregiving environment. The second presents the activities, instructs how to conduct them, and explains why they are helpful. Each chapter ends with questions to stimulate small group discussion regarding the principal points of the chapter and to encourage readers to apply and transfer the information to their own real-life situations.

Many traditional creative play themes and interactive activities and games are dying from disuse and fading from human memory. By referencing experts in the field of trauma and/or neuro-behavioral recovery such as Bruce Perry, Bessel van der Kolk, Karyn Purvis, David Cross, and Judith Bluestone, this book preserves entertaining and creative themes, games, and rhythmic play whose longstanding benefits will be lost if they pass into extinction. Further, this book brings a fresh approach to reintroducing these games and their benefits. It also encourages parents to help the children in their care come up with their own creative, pretend play that is fun and healing.

While the research and rationale for the activities through this book focus on helping traumatized children, the emphasis on therapeutic movement, physical activity, and real relationships can enrich the intellectual and socio-emotional development of all children.

Many caregivers need ideas to help get kids, traumatized or not, off their behinds and *on their feet* so they can physically experience creative play, fun activities, and real, live human interactions that better help them overcome life's challenges, connect to others, and build their brains.

Chapter 1

How Traumatic Stress Creates Maladaptive but Self-Protective Brain States

OR WHEN BAD THINGS HAPPEN TO SMALL PEOPLE

Fight-flight-freeze: When the brain registers "threat"

The small kitten, his heart beating rapidly, bit and clawed me as I struggled to bathe him in the kitchen sink. He was covered in grease from sleeping in the underbelly of parked cars and his coat was teeming with fleas. I had been feeding this little stray for a couple of days, and now it was time to give him a name, and a "forever" home. I decided to call him "Buddy." But before I could allow the filthy little thing to live with me in the house, I had to give him a bath. Though I washed him gently, Buddy fought the entire time. I consoled him as I scrubbed, assuring him that the only way I could let him stay inside and keep him safe from predators would be if he were clean. He didn't agree.

When Buddy's violent fussing and fighting didn't knock me off my course of action, he tried the escape tactic. He began flailing his limbs in rapid motion, but his feet just couldn't quite get a sure grip on the wet, soapy porcelain. By this time, his heart beat more wildly. I just held tighter and continued washing, all the while getting as wet as he was while I used my body to contain him. Throughout, I kept telling him how clean he would be and how good he would feel after his bath…as if he could understand what I was saying to him.

What Buddy did next surprised and scared me. He closed his eyes and just went limp. I no longer felt his heart pounding. I wasn't sure if I could feel it beating at all. I wondered if this little guy, who recently had come from such a rough place, had just died. Could he have had a heart attack or something? I rinsed him and wiped him dry, all the while calling his name again and again. I continued whispering "Buddy" and rocked him in my arms. Suddenly, he opened his eyes, looked at me, and began purring. When I set him down on the floor, he licked his paw and was ready to play.

It's important to look at how similar people are to animals. We can learn much from our fellow mammals, especially how they react to stress. Mammals and humans share common reactions to traumatic stress.

What Buddy demonstrated above was fight–flight–freeze, or survival response to traumatic stress, and then unexpected forgiveness when he was in his right mind. The situation started out bad…ended good. This first bath for a feral kitten who was willing to risk contact with humans to keep from starving to death was like a near-death experience for the little guy. By the way, I never bathed Buddy again. I didn't think I could put him through that experience a second time.

Since humans and other mammals, such as cats, share certain similar brain structures and brain responses (Figure 1.1), it is no accident that humans react to danger in much the same way animals do. Variations of such responses can be influenced by a human's personality, threat reaction style, and pre-experience of living life dangerously.

Figure 1.1 Humans and animals have similar stress response systems

Human and animal stress response systems

Buddy didn't think and plan what he was going to do, step by step, to get me to stop bathing him. Because he was no more than seven to nine weeks old, the thinking part of his brain wasn't that developed yet. Further, he hadn't been on the planet long enough to learn from other cats how to look pitiful and seek out sympathetic humans. He showed up at my house because he was hungry, and because other neighbors had been running him off. I may have been his last resort.

During the bath, a desperate, primal need to survive kicked in for him. Buddy's style of defensiveness, likely due to his species, gender, and personality, was to thrash, bite, scratch, and make scary noises in his throat. How did he know to do that? His feline genetic coding likely pre-programmed him to initially resist in the way he did. He reacted to clear, probable, and present danger. There was no thinking to it because he wasn't using that part of his brain. Instead, he went into his first automatic response: defense (fight) against something that for him seemed life threatening. It wasn't just soap and water, but soap and water administered by a human he had only recently met that frightened him.

When Buddy's fighting failed, he began evasive maneuvers: escape from the danger he couldn't stop from happening. I remember his heart beating even faster in this phase than it did in the initial fight phase. I wonder if the momentum or the desperation to live after one resistance maneuver fails involves even more of the body's determination and energy to survive. If you can't beat them, run from them.

When Buddy's evasive "flight" also failed, he had no other choices but to surrender or go into a freeze state, a state of non-deliberate, non-reaction. This is an avoidant "just give up, give in, prepare to die" phase because resistance is futile. His heartbeat slowed, his senses shut down, and he slipped into a state of submission, maybe even semi-consciousness, or dissociation. He checked out, became dead-like, and his body and mind checked back in when his brain told him that the danger was over, and he had survived. If death does come when one goes into a freeze state—lessening some of a shock to the system, alleviating pain, easing the terror—then the transition toward the afterlife might not be so bad after all.

Understanding three major divisions of the brain

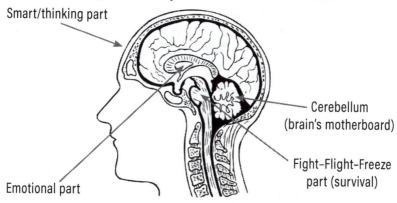

Smart/thinking part

Cerebellum
(brain's motherboard)

Fight-Flight-Freeze
part (survival)

Emotional part

Figure 1.2 Major divisions of the human brain

Physician and neuro-scientist Dr. Paul D. Maclean (1990) was the first to propose a triune (three-part) brain model of the major divisions of the human brain (Figure 1.2). It is an accepted scientific fact that the brain develops from the bottom of the head to the top of the head. The bottom of the head includes the fight–flight–freeze center, or survival response center, that is common among all living, breathing things. Inside the middle of the brain, where it cannot be seen unless the brain were split down the middle, is the seat of our emotions and feelings. On the top of the brain is the smart or thinking part of the brain. This is the highest part of the brain. The smart part of the brain is supposed to mature to a point that it controls or overrides strong emotions, feelings, and automatic responses that originate in the lower, more primitive parts of the brain like the emotional and fight–flight–freeze centers. This explanation of brain division and function is extremely simplified for the purpose of introducing the reader to basic, beginning neuroscience.

Consider the person who is reacting to a situation with what we commonly refer to as "road rage." When people have "lost their minds" and are cell-phone-recorded pounding the living daylights out of someone who cut them off in traffic or dinged their car door as they were opening theirs, their violent, over-the-top outburst likely wasn't planned or thought out. In other words, the smart part of the brain wasn't dictating their reaction, but the emotional and fight–flight–freeze centers were. Common sense should have told them to control themselves and act in a mature, grown-up fashion, but that system was not engaged. Their action was triggered by something in the deeper, darker, lower recesses of the brain that didn't get mediated by the higher, thinking part of that same organ.

The emotional and fight–flight–freeze centers of the brain don't think—they react. The job of the top, smart part, or highest part of the brain is to think and to control the emotional reactions of these lower centers. The highest part of the brain is about self-control. It uses critical thinking to plan, to figure things out, and to respond with good common sense. This part of the brain is supposed to mediate what's going on in the lower, non-thinking emotional or fight–flight–freeze centers of the brain, and just say "no" when necessary. When it doesn't or "can't" stop the lower parts of the brain from doing their emotional thing, then people can get caught up "in the heat of the moment" and say or do things that they, hopefully, will later regret.

I grew up with the term "hair-trigger" temper to describe someone who could easily and quickly "lose it" and become irrationally abusive or violent almost with no warning. The term did not refer to people who were under the influence of drugs and alcohol at the time of their outburst. Drugs and alcohol can cause the smart part of the brain to cease making good decisions, so people make stupid ones. Drugs and alcohol can also shut down the smart part of the brain completely so that the more non-thinking emotional and fight–flight–freeze centers of the brain are the systems in charge. How scary.

Even memory is a smart part function. When lower parts of the brain override the smart part, people often have no memory of what they said or did. That's because, during that reactive incident, the "boss" of the brain was nowhere to be found.

When the smart part (thinking part) of the brain does override the fight-flight-freeze stress response (survival) part of the brain

When a human is in a frightening situation and can still figure out a way to survive, then the smart part of the brain has kicked in to override the terror of the emotional part as well as the fight–flight–freeze part of the brain. In fact, a little bit of "fight" to survive is likely intact. So, the "fighting spirit" when bad things happen to good people is not a bad thing at all.

Most of us have heard about, witnessed or seen in movies or on TV how someone has played dead to keep from getting killed by another. An example would be the one living soldier on a battlefield of the dead whose only chance for survival was to not move a muscle. This isn't the same as the freeze state of submission. The soldier who consciously decides not to move and is able to control his body and his breath is thinking what to do, and how and when to do it. He's thinking how to look really, really dead.

Years ago, I worked in therapy with Vietnam veterans who had survived fire fights during that war, but had lost the battles. They had to play dead to keep from getting finished off by the enemy, who would look for survivors soon after the smoke had cleared. Some of the soldiers even told me that they had smeared the blood of nearby deceased soldiers onto their own bodies to complete the ruse. The smart part of the brain of the "pretending-to-be-dead" soldier was still very much in charge.

I remember when I was a young child and was scared to go to sleep at night in my birth home. I was especially frightened if my father was working the night shift at the local air force base. My mother, who suffered from mental illness, was the only adult in the home then, and I was afraid of her. If I went to sleep, then I could no longer protect myself from harm, nor escape from it, either. Traumatized children can have problems falling asleep and staying asleep if they developed, through practice, a nocturnal hypervigilance. When bad things happen to small children as they sleep, it is common for them to resist sleep. It is hard for the brain to let down its guard in children who haven't been safe when they rested. Their brain masters the art of survival: just fight sleep—it's safer that way. Hypervigilance becomes a habit that is hard to break, even when the child has been moved to the safety of trustworthy caregivers.

Though as a young child I couldn't identify it consciously, I knew, on some level, that I was in danger of a birth mother who could kill me in the night. This innate, unconscious knowledge caused me to resist sleep for as long as I could. My mind did not allow me to recognize that the danger during the sleeping hours was my mother. Instead, I imagined it was monsters in my closet, or snakes under my bed, or the worst enemy of all, the devil. Mother was supposed to be the earthly, physical representation of a loving God. She was supposed to protect me, love me, keep me safe...not be my worst, deadliest enemy. When my sister was born, my anxiety intensified. Beyond my own struggle to survive, I also sensed that I needed to keep my little sister alive as well.

I was predominantly a "fight" kid. "Fight" kids don't give up easily. It is fortunate when the oldest child in a violent home is the scrappiest. The younger, more helpless siblings stand a better chance of survival. Unconsciously, the scrappiest child may act as the decoy (as I did) in attempts to divert potential predators from their younger, smaller siblings. I suppose humans share that protective instinct with animals, too.

In time, I figured out a way to protect myself from harm, remain on the alert for danger to my little sister, and actually get some sleep. I did not, could not, go into a state of "freeze." I had to maintain awareness in the thinking, planning, smart part of my brain. Control of my senses enabled me to devise a safety plan and stick to it.

My plan was ingenious. I was sure it would protect my sister and me from harm. I slept on my back as if I were in a casket. I placed a Bible on my chest, my arms folded protectively over it in case I rolled over on my side as I slept. The Bible was my weapon against things that went bump in the night.

Any benevolent human being who could have walked into my room to see if I were asleep may wonder why on earth I would sleep in such a position. It was simple: if the devil thought I were dead, he would leave. I knew what dead people looked like in caskets. I had been to at least one funeral and certainly had seen my share of vampire movies. People who died in vampire movies had crucifixes placed on their chests in the caskets. The crucifixes were intended to keep those awful vampires away.

Unfortunately, because my family was Methodist, not Catholic, we had no crucifixes readily available. So, in my brilliant cause–effect thinking, I substituted what we did have handy—the Holy Bible. It had to be the next best weapon. I figured if Satan saw the Bible on my chest, he'd leave—fast!

It worked. I would fall asleep and wake up the next morning alive. I now think sleeping with a Bible on my chest also helped me at least want to believe in something that I couldn't see. I needed someone stronger than I was, stronger than anybody else, who could and would protect me. While still too young to read, I knew that someone named Jesus was somewhere in that Bible book. I had heard about him. I had seen a picture of Him with the little children. He appeared to really care for them. I had even been taught songs about Him, such as *Jesus Loves Me*. Still so young, I held to the belief that someone I wasn't able to see, who was in that Bible, could protect and watch over me when I slept. I could see my earthly father if he were home. But when he wasn't home, there was no physical body there to protect me. But with the Bible on my chest, Jesus was there. That belief was reinforced every morning when I awoke and realized I was still alive.

I remember opening the Bible to see if Jesus would pop out of it, like a little miniature figure in three-dimensional form. I cannot count the times I opened and closed that book hoping to see Him waving and smiling at me.

When the smart part (thinking part) of the brain doesn't override the fight-flight-freeze stress response system as well as it should: The "fight" continuum

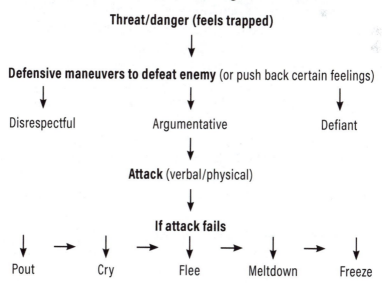

Figure 1.3 Common characteristics of children on "fight" continuum

Traumatized children tend to be hyper-aroused, hyper-vigilant, and hyper-alert unless they are already descending down the "freeze" continuum. They are focused on either defending themselves and others from potential threats or distracting and escaping from danger. Their little brains incite defensive maneuvers at the slightest provocation. Such provocations could be fast-moving little bodies that get too close, or not being able to see who is behind them. An even greater provocation is not getting what they want exactly when they want it, especially food. No one should touch a child who is descending down the "fight" continuum. This is the aggressive continuum (Figure 1.3). People who put their hands on children who are on this continuum run the risk of getting hurt.

The motto of a child in "fight": If you can't beat them, make them think you can.

When I was a child, I didn't want to be a girl. I identified more with boys. From my perspective, girls seemed weak and couldn't protect themselves, but boys seemed strong. Early observations showed me that, when boys were threatened, they often huffed and puffed and postured until they scared off whoever frightened them or, as they described it, "made them mad." Girls just cried, or worse—just stood there. Somebody had to protect girls.

During my youth, school started in the first grade, not kindergarten or pre-kindergarten. I recall my baby-booming first grade classroom crowded with at least 31 other children and only one teacher, my dear Miss Beetles. She was older, dark haired, small boned, but of ample girth. She was strong and could handle a classroom of fast-moving little people and actually teach those little people to read and write.

Besides always wanting to be by Miss Beetles' side, I craved her approval. Though I didn't realize it then, she reminded me of my paternal grandmother, who had kept me some of my early childhood. Grandma was a benevolent, higher force to be reckoned with.

My grandma always wore an apron and always carried a "switch" in that apron to wave around and remind children that they were to behave. A switch was a small, delicate branch from a bush that, if used, could sting the skin of a child's legs and, if used too harshly, could leave welts. I wasn't afraid of my grandma, and she never, ever used that switch to hurt me. But I just knew that robbers, scary monsters, and even Satan himself certainly had to be terrified of her and her switch.

Although Grandma was actually short, to me she was ten feet tall. I trusted her to defend me and keep me safe, and I knew she could do it. I'm sure I must have transferred the trust of my grandmother, as well as my love for her, to Miss Beetles.

As I recall it, I was reasonably well behaved in Miss Beetles' classroom when she was *in* the classroom. But the first few times she left during class to use the restroom, I immediately feared that my old enemy, Satan, would appear out of nowhere to attack all of us children in the class.

Without Miss Beetles' strong presence in the classroom to keep the devil away, I felt compelled to protect myself and my peers. With an aggressive show of strength, I could scare away the devil until Miss Beetles returned. As soon as she left, I would incite as many boys as I could to play a loud, boisterous game of out-of-control throw and catch with whatever we could pick up and toss.

I was large and in charge and ring-leading the boys, who were easily persuaded into misbehaving. I would throw anything I could find. Before long, many different items were sailing through the air, from all directions. It didn't matter what tables and chairs got knocked over, or which innocent bystanders were accidentally hit by flying debris. The game was on, and it was hard to stop the momentum of all "us" boys in action.

What had begun as a planned, well-thought-out course of action with at least some logic to it quickly descended into chaos. I soon forgot the whole purpose of my mission. If a boy didn't move fast enough or tried to sit down, I became aggressive. I growled. I stomped. I yelled. I tried to force the boy back onto his feet. I wanted to make him rejoin the madness.

I was so out of control I wouldn't see Miss Beetles through the large glass window as she stood outside the room, hands on her hips, observing the riot. I also never calmed down immediately when she would burst into the room, clapping her hands and demanding a cease fire. She knew I was commander of the troops. She watched me from the window. When she asked why I behaved as I did, I couldn't tell her why. I didn't know. I didn't understand why until later.

An inability to easily "pull it back" (up and out of the lower recesses, non-smart part of the brain) and return to a state of relative non-arousal (smart part of brain in charge) results when a child's brain has been assaulted too frequently by chronic, early stress. The child goes into hyper-arousal quickly. The better the brain is put together, the easier it is to turn on arousal or turn it off. The smart part of the brain has an easier job of controlling impulses, mood and emotions when it is in charge.

Strangely, I don't remember getting in trouble for what I'd start in Miss Beetles' classroom. I just remember that, eventually, when Miss Beetles went to the restroom she took me with her, securely holding my hand all the way.

I felt excited and happy to be with her. I got to walk with Miss Beetles to the restroom and back! I didn't realize that she held my hand because if she hadn't, she might have lost me. I didn't realize I was excitedly talking her head off during our round-trip excursion. But she knew. She knew something was up, something deeper than just misbehavior.

I recall how, like my grandma, she chuckled and watched me with a warm, twinkling gaze as I was chattering and skipping with my hand in hers. She liked me. That was all that mattered at the time. If she liked me, she would keep me safe. That's what my grandma did.

I truly believed that if Miss Beetles and I both were absent from the classroom of kids, the devil wouldn't come and hurt anybody. He would only come if I were in the room and Miss Beetles were not. Overly responsible children who hurt sure do take on a lot of grown-up duties—even when they don't have to.

If you are a teacher reading this story, don't ever underestimate the power you have in influencing a child's life. School might be the only safe place some children have. School may be the only place some children go where somebody cares enough about them to keep them safe, even if it is from themselves, as it was in my case.

I am blessed that Miss Beetles was in my life when she was. I look forward to seeing her again when I leave this earth. She was truly one of the angels God put along my path to get me where I am today.

When the smart part (thinking part) of the brain doesn't override the fight-flight-freeze stress response system as well as it should: The "flight" continuum

(Need is to escape from capture or at least from fearful feelings)

↓

Common diversionary tactics:

↓   ↓   ↓   ↓   ↓   ↓   ↓   ↓

Hide   Ignore   Make excuses   Chatter   Laugh   Act silly   Move a lot   Grovel

↓

Attempts to divert fail

↓   ↓   ↓   ↓   ↓   ↓

Beg/plead   Make deals   Blame   Lie   Whine/cry   Physically flee

↓

Escape fails

↓   ↓   ↓

Fight   Become hysterical   Freeze

Figure 1.4 Common characteristics of children on "flight" continuum

Like children in "fight" mode, children in "flight" mode are anxious and hyper-aroused. However, the symptoms of their anxiety are different.

Children in "fight" mode are more asserting and aggressive. While in "fight" mode they hate admitting being sad or, Heaven forbid, afraid. They will deny fear and call it anger. For them, anger is safer. Anger moves them forward to defend.

Conversely, children in "flight" mode (Figure 1.4) are more prone to avoid creating conflict, or at least be sneaky about creating it. They may not like to admit to being angry. To describe their anger, they may say they feel sad. Apparently for them, sadness is a safer emotion than anger.

Even though I was predominantly a "fight" kid, I knew when to choose my battles. In threatening situations that I had unconsciously sized up and knew I couldn't win, I switched over to "flight." The adults didn't understand me when I was in "flight" and likely found me most annoying. Many times I was accused of just wanting attention. It looked that way. I would move too fast and be too loud, too silly, and too disobedient—but not in a mean way. All I remember was that when my body or my mouth was in motion, I was distracted from fearful thoughts and even scarier feelings.

There are so many more "flight" evasive maneuvers. When threated, children in "flight" can cry, act silly, manipulate, blame, be passive, or become fake-phony. They can be the masters of excuse-making to get people off their trail when they start going down the "flight" continuum. They may develop nervous habits, like popping their knuckles or chronically yawning. They may become hyper-active or turn into "motor mouths," endlessly filling the air with unnecessary talking.

The motto of a person in "flight": If you can't beat them, throw them off your scent.

Many "flight" children have perfected either an expressionless countenance or an endlessly sweet sugar and spice smile. They may have mastered the art of running away, and then denying it. Their "yes" is more common than their "no." And their "yes" may not be dependable.

Here is an example of a predominantly "flight" child: Maribel was adopted by her family when she was four years old and became the oldest of five siblings. Her adopted mother, as in typical families with a larger number of children, had the most expectations of her. It is common to expect the oldest female of the brood to be mother's little helper. Maribel didn't want this role. As she got older, she was finally able to admit she was scared of failure, fearful that she wasn't strong enough for the job. It took a long time to get to that truth. She was too afraid to be honest. She made all kinds of excuses for not doing what she had been asked to do. Her "yes" meant nothing. She couldn't be trusted, and she grew to become quite sneaky.

Whatever expectation Mom had for Maribel, Maribel was sure to thwart. It didn't matter whether she was to ask the other children to gather their dirty clothes or to watch the little ones carefully in the back yard while Mom was cooking dinner. Maribel would never just say, "I'm not going to do it, and you can't make me." She would agree to do it and then just wouldn't.

When asked why she didn't do something she was supposed to, Maribel sometimes only responded by hanging her head and shrugging her shoulders. Other times, she responded with an excuse or an outlandish lie. She would say things like, "I didn't realize you were asking me to watch the kids in the back yard; I thought you were asking so and so to watch the kids." Or, "I did watch them, until so-and-so came out and I thought you told him to watch them, so I came back in the house." Maribel's mom stopped asking her why she hadn't done what she had agreed to do. And by the way, a "why didn't you do something" is the worst thing to ask a person in flight mode. It just pushes them deeper into flight... which could result in increased passive-aggressiveness or "freeze."

So, what caused Maribel to lie about why she didn't do the job she was asked to do? Was it passive-aggressive payback against Mom because she was mad at Mom about something—like asking her to be a helper? Was it because she didn't think she was fit for the job she was asked to do and didn't want to disappoint her superior because in her mind that was dangerous? Was it because she didn't want the job and didn't have the courage to ask her mom to ask someone else? Was it because she never felt like she fit into the family (translation: not good enough) and was going to prove it? Or all of the above? It sure is hard to get to the reason "why" with a "flight" kid. They may not know themselves. And they can be so evasive.

Really good "flight" kids can convince their inquisitors that they might be crazy, especially if their inquisitors are their parents. Being assertive and owning up to what they are up to just isn't their style. It takes courage to self-assess, and courage is one trait "flight" kids really have to work on.

Predominantly "fight" people hit conflict head on, and appear to be fearless about making people mad. It is easier for them to develop real courage once they get the smart part of their brains straightened out. Predominantly "flight" people are conflict avoidant and may try to avoid displeasing people. It is harder for them to develop real courage because they run so easily.

"Fight" people are typically regarded as assertive or aggressive while "flight" people are thought of as passive, passive-aggressive or passive-resistant. As a therapist, I have seen through the years that it is much easier to teach mildly afflicted "fight" people to tone it down. In other words, if the smart parts of their brains can become relatively operational in mediating impulses, desires, and reactions coming from the lower reaches, then they are much easier to habilitate than "flight" people. They at least have courage and strong will. I understand better where "fight" people are coming from because, if they know what they are thinking, they will tell me.

"Flight" kids have to practice courage and assertiveness and find out they won't get eaten if they tell someone who is safe the truth of how they feel. Someone may need them one day to protect them, or to go get help. They have to be able to act, to do something, in order to help not only themselves out of a real threatening situation, but to help someone else as well.

When the fight-flight arousal continuums fail: The "freeze" continuum

Threat/danger

↓

Fight-flight attempts fail

↓

Initial system shutdown: beginning dissociation
(Person feels "foggy," even drowsy, less alert; moves slower; finds it harder for speech to flow; may pop knuckles or yawn; not as alert; may look ADD-like; people and what's happening now seem farther away; pain not as distinct; feels emotionally numb; person is not as aware of time and body in space)

↓

Dissociation
(Body present, but person is not; eyes are open but person is unresponsive; may have lack of wareness or memory from this period; "blank" look on face; no feeling of pain)

↓

Shutdown complete
(Unconsciousness, person appears to have fallen asleep or has fainted)

Figure 1.5 Uninterrupted "freeze" continuum

In the freeze state, the person has no control of their brain (Figure 1.5). This state of "being dead" is also referred to as a dissociative state. In this state, the pulse drops, blood pressure decreases, breath becomes so shallow it's hardly noticeable. The person in this state may perceive others as if they were at a distance, and not quite real.

There were circumstances in my childhood when I had to go into this "freeze" state. These would be times when my mother had physically trapped me, and I had no way of getting away from her. She would distort her face, spew and spit loud, growling, angry sounds along with threatening epitaphs. She would corner me. I couldn't stop her; I couldn't get away from her. As she would get more and more out of control and kick me, hit me, slap me, and bang my head against whatever she could bang it into, I would begin to go away. It felt as if I were merely observing, not experiencing what was going on.

My struggling, crying, pleading, and attempting to cover my face or protect my head with my hands just made her worse. Resistance was futile. I surrendered and became motionless, and most of all silent. The blows against my body stopped hurting. I ceased being terrified and felt nothing at all. I could hear my head being hit against the wall, as if from a distance, but I couldn't feel anything. And best of all, my mother's voice, her rantings and railings, would become farther and farther away, even though she was pulverizing me. Then I would remember nothing. I didn't know when she would stop. Had she knocked me unconscious or had I completely dissociated and gone to the extreme end of the "freeze" continuum into la-la land? I'll never know.

When the fight–flight responses to threat fail, the stress response system is overwhelmed and a system shutdown is imminent. When the brain is in a system shutdown mode, the body is at its most defenseless. The brain is preparing for death.

There is an immediate benefit to the "freeze" state: lack of memory or awareness for a mind (located in the smart part of the brain) that can't handle what happened. It experiences no terror, just a nothingness. The problem is, for those with "freeze" state experience, the brain and body can dissociate into a state of "freeze" in similarly triggered circumstances. And the circumstance may be benign such as being called on in class to answer a question, for example. In the freeze state, memory is impaired. If memory does start coming back, it's hard to know if the incident really happened or not. The line becomes blurred between fact and fiction.

CHAPTER QUESTIONS

1. Is your child predominantly a fight, flight, or freeze kind of child? On what do you base your opinion?

2. What about yourself? Are you predominantly a fight, flight, or freeze kind of person? What do you do when you are backed into a corner?

3. What bothers you the most about your child's behavior? Why?

4. Does your child dissociate? How can you tell?

5. When were some occasions when you had to override panic or shut-down, to act to keep yourself or others safe?

6. Can you think of times when people or animals have been triggered into odd "flight" or "freeze" responses during a crisis? For example, firefighters know to look under furniture, especially beds, for animals and small children when they are rescuing inhabitants from houses that are on fire.

7. How does military training train the "flight/freeze" out of someone?

Chapter 2

How Movement, "Real-World" Play, and Non-Virtual Relationships Can Build Brains, Better Minds, and Bolster Bonds

OR WHAT I LEARNED FROM PLAYING SODOM AND GOMORRAH WITH BARBIE DOLLS

When Sodom and Gomorrah were destroyed

When the morning dawned, the angels urged Lot to hurry, saying, "Arise, take your wife and your two daughters who are here, lest you be consumed in the punishment of the city."

Genesis 19:15

So it came to pass, when they had brought them outside, that he said, "Escape for your life! Do not look behind you nor stay anywhere in the plain. Escape to the mountains, lest you be destroyed."

Genesis 19:17

But his wife looked back behind him, and she became a pillar of salt.

Genesis 19:26

Following his wife's transformation, Lot had to take his two daughters and go, leaving his wife behind. She was turned into a pillar of salt for disobeying God. God took care of the problem. Lot and his daughters moved on without her.

I played Sodom and Gomorrah with Barbie dolls when I was a young child: over and over again. Ken was Lot, my Barbie was the oldest daughter, and my sister's Barbie was the younger. A doll which was not from the Barbie clan (but from a company that was in competition with the makers of Barbie and pals) was Lot's wife. She had bad hair. I robed my entourage with scraps of material that I pieced together myself with safety pins. They had to look like the pictures in the children's Bible that I had. I turned a small rock candy bag into a food bag for Lot to throw over his shoulder and carry on his journey. People had to eat. I filled the candy bag with small rocks to be the potatoes he and his family would surely need. (Children who have gone hungry before often ensure their food needs are taken care of in their creative pretend play.)

Lot guided his family up the ottoman in our living room that represented the hill that certainly the family had to ascend in order to escape from the doom, gloom, fire, and destruction below them in Sodom and Gomorrah—the twin cities that God had set on fire for the sins of its people. The "family" couldn't bring the mother with them. She was one of those sinners. She proved her unreliability by looking back. She was removed. God took care of her.

My conscious mind had no idea the statement I was making with my pretend play. It didn't matter that I didn't understand what the story of Sodom and Gomorrah really meant, nor that I may have confused some of the details. My subconscious mind, however, knew what it was doing. That particular pretend play gave the feeling part of my brain some peace and confidence that things would all work out in the end. Somehow, I was beginning to understand the entity that I couldn't see, but was told to trust. Was I making a three-dimensional prayer for God to answer without realizing that was what I was doing? Maybe. Did I subconsciously want God to punish my mother? Another maybe. What mattered is that the repetitive play on the topic of Lot's escape from Sodom and Gomorrah added to my resiliency, my peace of mind, and my sense of protection and hope. I didn't need to know the truth of what I was playing.

I'm sure I had overheard my mother's people urging my father to take my little sister and me and just go. They stressed the fact that my mother had always been crazy and that she was too dangerous to be a mother to two small needy children. He was away from the home at least nine hours a day. Much could happen during the time he wasn't there to protect us, and keep us quiet, so we wouldn't disturb or upset our mother. But my father believed that when you dug your grave, you lay in it, and he did. He wouldn't leave her and he wouldn't let us go live with relatives to raise us permanently, only for short periods of time when things got really bad. Whenever mother stabilized somewhat, because we weren't around her doing what small children do, we went back home. Then, the cycle of birth home to relatives' home and back would begin all over again.

In the hours alone at my mother's home, inside the house, waiting for my father to come back, I had to be quiet, not draw any attention to myself, not have any needs that adults had to tend to. That could be deadly. I was scared. I couldn't show my anxiety, insecurity, and fear via hyper-active aberrant movement, fighting with my sister, chattering, singing, or making noises. I was smart and had learned through painful experience to discipline myself to hold it together. Mother's response could be lethal. So, when I had to stay inside the house, a most unsafe place to be, I played with miniature figures (I called them "my little animals"), and with Barbie dolls. It wasn't just to bide my time, but to creatively calm my anxiety and give me constructive movement that distracted me from fear. As well, I needed to have a sense of control over something where I could make end the way I wanted. I needed something hopeful to believe in—even if the interpretation of my repetitive creative play wasn't widely socially acceptable nor understood.

My creative, three-dimensional, solitary pretend play was my comfort, my solace, and my salvation.

I didn't see what my Sodom and Gomorrah play truly meant at the time, but my subconscious did. The brain develops and habilitates through targeted experience and repetition. Through my Sodom and Gomorrah play, I practiced hope that one day I would be rescued from a crazy woman and a crazy home that was imploding in flames and destruction in a figurative way. That particular pretend play also helped me nurture a beginning belief in a benevolent power of protection that I could not see. In order for that new belief to grow, it had to be practiced in order to become perfect. I practiced and practiced.

What is played or witnessed repetitively is training for the brain

In creative pretend play, what the body practices, whether solitarily or in group, the brain adopts. What is practiced then becomes a part of one's conscious and subconscious. What is taken in, passively and repetitively, with the eyes, has a great impact on the formation of the beliefs of the subconscious part of the brain. What is not only taken in with the eyes but also practiced by the body has an even greater impact on nurturing a force for good or a force for destruction in relationships with the self and with others. Think of the implications of this truth and consider how young minds are impacted by television, computer games, or other forms of screen violence.

The exposure to and the participation in screen violence, especially when the good guys don't win, further internalizes a burning, imploding figurative Sodom and Gomorrah into the brains and minds of the young viewers and active players who indulge in those activities. Children who come from hurting places should never be allowed to escape into screen violence after they have been physically rescued from the figurative Sodom and Gomorrah of their traumatized background. Screen violence prevents them from ever leaving Sodom and Gomorrah at all.

The non-smart parts of the brain are unable to differentiate fact from fiction. If there is violence, gloom, and doom on the screen, then it is still happening, live, as far as the brain is concerned, right in front of the viewer. The adrenalin rush, the fear, the anxiety, is real to the fight–flight–freeze center of the brain. The body still reacts as if it is under threat. If the viewer becomes a participant, either through violent physical or computer game play, then the person gets personal experience and practice in how to carry out violence and make it real. Screen violence is not habilitative. It impedes all good intentions to help heal a brain traumatized by events and people.

Constructive, creative, pretend play helps the smart (highest) part of the brain become a better boss

Constructive, creative, pretend play is therapeutic. It can help children improve their sense of well-being and resiliency. As long as the play is positive (instead of destructive, selfish, or hurtful with no beneficial outcome for anyone involved), then there is no need for adult intervention or restructuring of the play.

What is practiced becomes perfect. Make sure children are practicing what the soul needs.

Via pretend play, children should become active, problem-solving participants of their own journey through the physical world. It feeds them socio-emotionally. Their play helps them build character, self-identity, self-responsibility, confidence, cause–effect thinking, and courage.

Positive pretend play helps children make some sense out of the world in which they live, giving them a feeling of control over something. It reinforces safety—security, trust, hope, and resilience. Pretend play should help children practice trusting others who should be trusted, and determine who they can depend on and who they can't. It should help children learn how to share, jointly problem-solve, be helpers to others, and otherwise internalize the Fruit of the Spirit (or Holy Spirit) as stated in Galatians 5:22–23.

The non-smart, lower part of the brain must be exercised and/or habilitated so the smart part of the brain can do its job better

A well-functioning non-smart part of the brain enables the smart part of the brain to adjust the attitude or the mind more easily. Children who have healthily operating lower brains have healthily operating thinking brains. These kids can choose their attitudes; the attitude is not chosen for them by the emotional or fight–flight–freeze centers. If a child decides not to change a poor attitude or behavior, then that child makes a "won't" (don't want to) decision. Such children have the ability to foresee the outcome of their behavior and change it if need be. If they continue down the wrong path, then they have decided that freedom, liberty, and the rewards of being likable and fun to be around aren't worth it at the moment or that it is much more lucrative to test the caregiver's patience and/or ability to follow through on a consequence. That child can think, plan...and think and plan well.

Behavioral modification programs that target desirable behaviors and offer rewards or consequences just don't work that well with lower brain issues or "can't" (just can't help it) kids. The kids may want those rewards but just "can't" get there because the smart part of their brains can't control their lower emotional and fight–flight–freeze centers that well. Rewards for good behavior and consequences for undesirable behavior work much better with in need-of-an-attitude-adjustment-only "will" or "won't" (choosing not to cooperate) kids.

Children who easily dysregulate, easily get on the "fight" continuum and become argumentative, oppositional, and melt down easily could be "can'ts" instead of "won'ts." The lower, more reactive, non-thinking centers of the brain could be the parts of the brain which are unfortunately in charge.

When is it a "can't" and when is it a "won't"?

When is a child's behavior something they can't control? When is it something they can, but choose (decision making in place) not to control? In the latter case, they really haven't lost their minds; they can pull it back at any time, and their recovery from their supposedly wall-eyed fit is just a little too fast. In fact, the complete recovery was perfectly timed to when they got what they wanted.

To make confusion even more confusing, there are children who start out on an in-control crying jag because they haven't gotten what they wanted, then work terrifically hard at being upset to the point that they drive themselves down the road into a dysregulated, no way back, wall-eyed meta meltdown. In other words, they started off as a "won't," but ended up a "can't."

Children who don't have really good control of their brains can get stuck in feeling states, like someone with their foot nailed down on a car accelerator. When kids get "stuck," they can move with lightning speed from "won't" to "can't" in a matter of seconds.

If children who are developmentally capable of walking are unable to pull themselves out of a tantrum, on their own, in a reasonable amount of time, and in fact are a threat to property, or human or animal life, then there is a problem. Alternately, if children can stop the spiraling downward before sending normal adults into fight–flight–freeze, then the brain is practicing self-control. The brain and body learn what they practice, and practice makes perfect. If a child is allowed to spiral downward time after time into the dark, deep stress-response recesses of the brain, where they can't pull up and out of it on their own, and they get no help from others to pull out of it, then they practice dysregulation. Dysregulation is what becomes perfect. If a child is out of control, and they are put in their room to trash it, they are practicing not just brain dysregulation but human destruction.

When kids who don't have great brain regulation get stuck in a downward "fight" continuum, they are truly not in their right minds. In fact, they aren't in their minds at all. Can they be turned around? Can an intervention that does not include psychotropic medication happen before they reach the point of no return? Hopefully, yes. But one has to be observant. Read the brain state properly, and intervene before a child becomes "stuck" in a downward spiral and before they are able to pull back out of it without help. Strive to intervene before a child gets "stuck."

It is sometimes difficult to determine when a child is truly moving toward the point of no return or just being stubborn, hard-headed, and wanting what they want when they want it. In other words, sometimes they're just testing limits, boundaries, and adults' patience. They are in complete control of themselves, no brain dysregulation problems. The tell-tale sign is how fast they can pull it back upon realization of imminent consequences for not accepting "no." We have an old Texas expression that caregivers would say to children who were being unhappy and unpleasant to be around because they didn't get what they wanted, "You can get glad in the same pants you got mad in."

What could be the real sources of the "can'ts" and "won'ts" that we see?

Of course, when children are tired, hungry, sick, or developmentally at the age when they get over-stimulated easily, they may slip into the non-smart, lower parts of the brain and be temporarily unpleasant to be around; however, children who experienced poor nutrition, alcohol, cigarettes, drugs, or chronic stress in their mothers' wombs had their lower brain centers set up for disturbance before they were even born. In fact, too much in utero stress causes the fight–flight–freeze center of the unborn baby's brain to be overactive upon birth. If this center is overactive, then the emotional part of the brain is also overactive.

Mothers who were chronically under a tremendous amount of stress while pregnant can also have babies who have an overactive stress response system and problems with anxiety that make them go too quickly into fight–flight–freeze states, just as their moms experienced while pregnant.

When a child is born, there is a critical developmental period for brain growth. Even if the in utero period were a good one, an early post-utero period filled with too much stress wreaks havoc with the continued "good" growth of the brain. There are early post-birth factors which negatively impact a baby's lower brain systems. Some of these factors are too many changes in caregivers, neglectful or abusive caregivers, mentally ill caregivers, or super-depressed or drug addicted/alcoholic moms who are unable to provide consistent good care for a baby's rapidly growing body, brain, and mind. A child needs a safe, predictable, stable, healthy first year of life after birth, so the lower part of the brain doesn't create a child who is predominantly a "can't" instead of a "won't."

Not all breaks in caregiving are the parents' faults. Children can have illnesses which cause intrusive surgeries and hospitalizations. Children can be born prematurely with lengthy neonatal intensive care unit (NICU) stays and their skin may be too sensitive or their bodies too fragile to support a lot of human touch until they get a little older. It's not the mother's fault. Sometimes, stuff just happens.

Sometimes a child is trying to navigate through their world without the best lower brain package to do so. Sometimes a child just needs adult guidance, intervention, and practice in brotherly love, putting others first, being a good friend, and practicing respect for others.

All children need movement and neuro-behavioral play that build up and strengthen the lower parts of the brain upon which the highest part of the brain builds. A child who was traumatized early on and displays strong "can't" characteristics commonly shows distress in the following neurosensory/neuro-behavioral areas and must have activities that will positively impact these areas, so that the smart part of the brain can operate with greater ease and fewer problems. Much of the following information came from my training with Judith Bluestone, creator of the HANDLE Approach (Holistic Approach to Neurodevelopment and Learning Efficiency) and author of the book *The Fabric of Autism* (2004).

Vestibular system

This system is essentially the inner ear, the part of the ear that commonly suffers from ear infections. Its job is not just to help in the hearing process but also to read all movement inside and outside of the body. That's why it's so important in balance. Lack of balance and dizziness can be one of the signs that something is going on with this system that shouldn't be. It is the initial processor of all movement, in and outside of the body. It helps information reach the cerebellum, which may be the brain's motherboard, in the lower, non-thinking part of the brain.

The vestibular system must read all movement that can be picked up by the senses. This could be as minute as the inner flow of blood or the blinking of the eyes to the outer movement of a rapid swarm of noise-making, arm-flapping little children in motion.

This system must be strong because it supports basically everything we do. If there is much going on, such as people talking, bodies moving, dogs barking, trains passing, fans blowing, televisions blaring, and doors slamming, then a weak, compromised vestibular system will shut down and stop supporting the higher brain functions. When that happens, people can easily go into a state of fight–flight–freeze and have trouble keeping it together emotionally.

An efficient vestibular system helps us manage stress. As people get older, so do their vestibular systems. Older people or seniors have more trouble with balance, multi-tasking, memory, and patience with fast-moving little entities such as children. As people move into old age, so do their vestibular systems. Brain functions that the smart part of the brain must modulate need a strong vestibular system for support.

Proprioceptive awareness

Proprioception joins forces with other systems of the brain and body to tell us where we are in time and in space. It is directly dependent on the vestibular system. When a person has a proprioceptive deficit, that person typically depends on the eyes to indicate where the body and its various visible parts are because they just don't have a good "feel" for where the body is—or isn't.

Problems in this area can be associated with the "freeze" continuum and the protective brain state of dissociation. The proprioceptors of a person in a dissociated state are in some degree of "off."

Proprioceptors are the receptors for the self. They are primarily in the connective parts of the body such as the joints. Knuckle poppers are popping their knuckles for a reason. It's a way to keep proprioception "turned on" and stop the brain's descent into the "freeze" state due to too much stress.

People with significant proprioceptive issues will have trouble connecting with their own bodies. A proprioceptive deficit limits the ability to be self-aware, which always precedes true self-identity.

A significant proprioceptive deficiency can cause problems in being other-aware. This is because people with proprioceptive deficiencies may be unsure of where they end and where something or someone else begins. This can create problems with emotional and physical boundaries. Examples of physical boundary problems could be how close to stand to someone, how much room is needed to pass someone, or even how to draw something that fits nicely and proportionately on the paper. Examples of emotional boundary problems could be the projecting of one's own feelings onto someone else. For example, if a person is feeling sad and needs a hug, that person may go up to another person and say, "You look like you need a hug," and then reach out to embrace that person, whether or not the person even wants a hug.

Children who were severely neglected during the early part of life after birth may have proprioceptive systems that are not working properly, since neglected children typically aren't held enough. Caregiver touch and movement help activate this system via the vestibular system during infancy. Often, past neglectful infancy, these children are the ones who caregivers describe as "clinging vines."

"Oh, if my body were covered in Velcro, this child would be fabulously happy," is a common statement I've heard from caregivers who have children who try to cling to them all the time like little monkeys.

If a child was physically or sexually abused, then the proprioceptors, which previously may have been working effectively, could have deactivated because of the physical pain and physical shock to the body. When children are unable to tolerate what is happening to them and are unable to escape from what is happening to them, a survival option is to dissociate or disconnect from time, space, and body. The child could be walking around in a perpetual state of "freeze."

One of my evaluatory testing procedures is to have children stretch an arm out and point at my left ear. When they point at their own ear or seem confused as to where to point and are flailing their arms about pointing at their own various body parts, that gives me a clue as to how aware they are of their own body, where they are in time and space, and where I am. People who are not aware of where their own physical body is or where another's physical body is in time and in space have a hard time identifying what they are feeling. They also have a hard time identifying how they have made someone else feel. Awareness of where the body is in time and in space precedes awareness of the feeling states of the self and of others.

Someone with a proprioceptive deficit can have trouble differentiating where the voice they hear is coming from. Are they having a thought (inside the head)? Are they having an auditory hallucination (outside the head)?

Differentiation (Bluestone 2003–6)

Brain circuits have to be organized enough to support regulation of the emotions, control impulses, and help the smart part of the brain sustain attention and make good decisions. Mature differentiation is the precursor to good interhemispheric integration, or the ability of the two sides of the smart part of the brain to communicate with each other. An ADHD (attention deficit hyper-activity disordered), fast-moving, emotionally dysregulated child may likely have a problem with differentiation.

Mature differentiation should be the result of proper reflex integration in infancy. Reflex integration is the developmental inhibition of primitive reflexes. An example of a primitive reflex would be the way newborns automatically wrap their little fingers around a person's finger when that person puts his finger into their little hands. There is no thought to it, even though we would like to think that there is. That reflex has to stop turning on automatically, so the infant's fingers can start responding to what the growing smart part of the brain wants them to do—which could range anywhere from touching Mama's face with the finger tips to pinching the dog.

Perhaps a child experienced too much stress as an infant and necessary reflexes, such as the whole-body startle response (MORO reflex), didn't integrate or inhibit (mature) as it should have because the brain was in a state of heightened anxiety too much of the time. The startle response is a reflex that causes someone to jump or startle at a sudden provocation: a door opening, someone quietly walking up from the rear, or the sound of a train in the distance, for example. Babies startle with their whole body. If that infantile reflex doesn't integrate because of too much early stress, then the older child or even the adult will still startle with an involuntary whole body response, rather than just turning the head, and perhaps flexing the shoulders, to see what happened.

When the startle response is "on" too much of the time due to too much stress, then the brain is in the fight–flight–freeze center too much of the time as well. "A stressed brain doesn't learn," said Judith Bluestone. A stressed brain that is spending too much time in the survival part of the brain or fight–flight–freeze center has difficulty supporting the smart part of the brain. A well-supported smart part of the brain is necessary for good self-control and mood regulation.

If a child moves unnecessary body parts to perform simple tasks, then differentiation may be immature. If there is body overflow movement to body parts that are supposed to be still when an unassociated physical task is performed, then differentiation could be a problem. For example, if a child moves his head while reading the written word, or sticks his tongue out while concentrating on a task that requires movement only of the fingers, or moves his feet when he should just be moving his hands, then differentiation may not be mature. How the body moves and suppresses the movement of unnecessary body parts is the best reflector of how well the brain is organized.

If the smart part of the brain can switch on or off a behavior or switch on or off a desire or a thought, or even a mood state, then one should have fairly good differentiation.

Interhemispheric integration (Bluestone 2003-6)

Ideally, this integration occurs when the right and left hemispheres of the smart part of the brain communicate well with each other. The communication between the two hemispheres of the front higher part of the brain should go back and forth or switch rapidly. Good interhemispheric integration builds on good mature differentiation.

Interhemispheric integration allows a person to focus on more than one thing at a time (like walk, talk, and chew gum at the same time, as the saying goes). It also helps people transition with ease from one activity or thought to another without getting "stuck." Getting stuck on thoughts can lead one down the road to "stinking thinking," which could include excessively focusing on frightening or depressing thoughts, or nagging thoughts that won't go away. Sticky interhemispheric switching is the foundation for chronic fretting, worrying, and obsessing, and addiction to behaviors or substances. Good interhemispheric integration allows good cause-effect or common sense thinking to happen. It allows the brain to shift off of disturbing or compulsive thoughts and better regulate emotions and feelings.

The brain works in an interdependent manner: Systems and functions build, one upon the other

When neurosensory or neuro-behavioral systems don't work well in cooperation with each other, nor work well on their own, problems arise. It's just too easy for the inefficient brain to descend into fight–flight–freeze states or even into a state of confusion if key neurosensory/neuro-behavioral functions of the brain aren't working as they should. If one or more key neurosensory functions such as vestibular, proprioceptive, differentiation, or interhemispheric integration is operating at a deficit, then a child's less than optimal behavior may be a "can't" (brain problem) instead of a "won't" (attitude, mind, or smart part of the brain only) problem.

Figure 2.1 provides a better visual on what could be going on in there (the brain and/or mind) that is demonstrated in a child's behavior.

When Is It a "Can't" and When Is It a "Won't"?

Behavior	Possible "Can't" Reasons	Possible "Won't" Reasons
Child is fidgeting and not sitting still.	1. Anxious (Flight Continuum). 2. Immature differentiation. 3. Has been sitting too long for developmental age and needs a break.	1. Bored. 2. Needs to practice self-discipline and brain supports the practice.
Child demonstrates poor up-close eye contact with others.	1. Anxious when people are too close (Flight Continuum). 2. Vestibular system does not support up-close eye contact with others.	1. Child not taught to look people in their eyes and just needs practice and reminders. 2. Child not looking someone in the eyes due to anger, embarrassment or shame.
Child bumps into people.	1. Immature differentiation. 2. Proprioceptive deficiency. 3. Compromised vestibular system. 4. Vision problems.	1. Child is in too much of a hurry and being careless. 2. Child focused on something else instead of where body is. 3. Intentional bullying.
If child is watching TV, child doesn't respond when called.	Child over-focuses on task and blocks all else out.	Child can hear name being called but is ignoring the caller.
Child argues incessantly when told "no."	Interhemispheric stickiness an issue: child can't turn off the desire for what child wants, nor the arguing.	Child knows to pester caregiver until caregiver gives in.

Note: *Always first try to figure out if the behavior could possibly be a "can't" before deciding if it's a "won't." It takes longer to change a "can't" than it does a "won't."*

Figure 2.1 Can't and won't chart

Interpreting the sources of the symptoms: What the diagnostic labels may really mean

Certainly, children who are on the fight–flight–freeze continuums get behavioral labels that pertain to the symptoms, not the sources. For example, a child who is hypo-vestibular (moving too fast too much of the time) is frequently labeled ADHD (Figure 2.2). On the contrary, a child who is hyper-vestibular (moving too slowly too much of the time) could be labeled ADD (attention deficit disordered). What really could be happening is that the child is somewhere along the flight–freeze continuum. The ADHD behaviors could be indicative of "flight" or hyper-arousal. The ADD behaviors could be indicative of a child somewhere along the "freeze" continuum who is sinking deeper into dissociation. A child who easily slips into oppositional defiance could be on the "fight" hyper-arousal continuum. An oppositionally defiant child would rather refuse than cooperate (or fight than switch?). This kind of child gets stuck on "no" and will die on that hill.

Common Causes of ADHD Symptoms

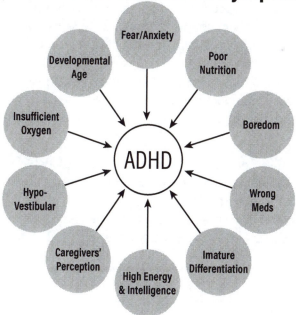

Figure 2.2 Common causes of ADHD

Too many kids who are disruptive or who push away the ones who are trying to love them get diagnosed with attachment disorder, conduct disorder, oppositional defiant disorder, or, my personal favorite, intermittent explosive disorder. People too frequently judge these children who have lower brain issues calling the shots, so to speak, as "won'ts" (attitude problem) when they really may be "can'ts" (brain just not working right). Too many uninformed caregivers become angry with these children and end up in judgment against them. They perceive the children's crummy behavior as a personal offense, as if the "can't" child is out to get them.

Neuro-behavioral play strengthens the neurosensory systems that support the smart part of the brain

Play should also be neuro-behaviorally enhancing. In order for play to be neuro-behaviorally enhancing or habilitative, it must be "real world," or experienced in the body as physical movement.

Play that is neuro-behaviorally enhancing has to impact base systems, or the "can't" lower brain systems that the smart part of the brain ("will" or "won't" centers) depend on to function efficiently. For children who were traumatized in utero, early post-utero, or both, play must be neuro-behaviorally habilitative for the brain. For any child who is participating in physical play, the movement of the physical body must be enjoyable. The brain systems and functions that can be helped by neuro-behavioral play will accept the movement as therapeutic if the movements are pleasurable instead of frightening.

Note: If a game or activity is too developmentally difficult for a child, either choose a simpler game or activity or make the intended game or activity more developmentally appropriate, so that the child doesn't become too frustrated. If a child becomes too stressed and frustrated because of the play, then the play is no longer therapeutic. A stressed brain doesn't learn. A brain that experiences fun, learns faster.

"Swing the Statue"

As a child I loved playing "Swing the Statue" in a group play setting. In some parts of the English-speaking world, I understand it was called "Statues." We played this game outside, on the grass, and the game was competitive in nature. The game required someone's father, mother, or older and stronger sibling be the "swinger." The children gathered near the swinger to be swung around, one by one. The swinger was required to grasp a child by the hands and swing the child around and around and maybe off the feet, slowly releasing in a manner that did not cause the child to fly through the air like a flapping bird. In other words, one was safely and securely released so as to stand a better chance of a soft and painless landing either on the feet or at least on the knees, side or bottom.

The children were also swung and released in a manner that did not cause them stress or anxiety, and in a manner that they could control the speed and movement of their physical body upon touch down. Some children would spin and pretend to stagger around as if they were drunk. Some would pretty quickly settle into a non-moving position that was fairly easy for them to keep.

Of course, in those days, because play and movement was what we had to do to entertain ourselves, our bodies were fairly physically fit. Most of us had relatively good balance and we were generally pretty well coordinated since we practiced movement as much as we did. It was still important that the swinger was attuned to what we needed. The swinger could tell how much movement we could tolerate by our facial expressions or our excitement or slight hesitancy to play the game.

Trust in the swinger and trust in our own body's ability to move through time and space mattered. Our courage to test the unknown and our desire to be in relationship with our peers mattered. So there was a socio-emotional or affective quality to this game. The game helped to build bonds and bolster relationships (and perhaps the enjoyment of dizziness).

The biggest socio-emotional boost I probably got from the game was being in control of my "freeze" state. Here was a safe place, away from my violent mother, where I could decide how and for how long I would freeze. I could stay fully aware. I got to experience a freeze in pleasure, not a freeze as a result of desperation. The game helped give me some sort of a sense of control over my young life which added to my resiliency.

Also, many of the children, myself included, wanted to get laughs out of the others, so we made our landings as dramatic and as physically contorted as possible with as many added sound effects as we could make. In order to stay in the game, the "swingees" had to remain frozen and silent in whatever position they landed because statues don't move and don't make noises. As children moved, they were called out and had to exit from the game. They then became the spotters to catch the other children who moved.

Key neurosensory, neuro-behavioral functions practiced in "Swing the Statue" in a neuro-sequential manner (one brain system skill building upon the other) were the following.

VESTIBULAR SYSTEM

The inner ear received controlled information in a therapeutic manner (not too much and not too little) regarding where the body was in time and in space. This is because the children assisted the swinger in their physical travel through space, and could determine how they landed. Once on the ground, the children were in control of the spinning and the speed that ultimately brought them to their final body resting place. The brain could read and process the movement so that proprioception could be supported.

PROPRIOCEPTION

Children had to practice focusing on where their body parts were in order to know where they were in time and in space. Plus, children had to work on falling into a position that could be held by the body for a relatively long time as far as child-time goes. The game emphasized body part awareness, which supported self-awareness.

DIFFERENTIATION

Children had to practice isolating body parts and focusing on keeping them still which practiced the brain's on/off switch. Children had to fight the impulse to move, scratch their nose, sneeze, or laugh, for example. In this game, they had to practice impulse control as well as mood regulation. Spotters tried to make the statues laugh or lose their postures by acting silly. The statues had to practice impulse control and focus. Every child wanted to be the last one standing (or kneeling or sitting or posed in some contorted yogic position) in this competitive game.

INTERHEMISPHERIC INTEGRATION

Children pre-planned how their body would travel through space and land in a relatively easy position to maintain (or to make others laugh). This planning exercised the smart part of the brain. Children had to think. When children acted as spotters, they had to be able to focus and multi-task in order to catch the statues making subtle body movements and then make their case that they had caught someone moving.

What follows are some samples of socio-emotional and neuro-behavioral play activities from my childhood or from my therapy practice. Feel free to enjoy or to reminisce or both!

Pretend play themes which help the mind practice courage, resiliency, and the Fruit of the Spirit (as well as some sense of control in a goofy, old world)

1. Good wins over evil: Or how bad situations turn out fine in the end

Examples:

- Miniature figure play where good guys win in the end

    - Good dinosaurs versus bad dinosaurs

- Group play where teams of good guys win over the bad guys

    - Armed forces or military play

- Group play with members escaping from danger games

    - Hide and go seek or chasing games

2. Courage and resiliency play: Or even I can make a difference

Examples:

- Hero-themed play where individual players perform extraordinary feats of bravery to rescue others from seen or unseen menaces

    - Miniature figure rescue operations

- – Cowboy or cowgirl rescues farm animals from a natural disaster or a natural enemy
- – Action figure search and rescues
- – Firemen, policemen, or Spiderman keeping good guys safe
- Group play where individuals rescue the helpless
  - – Impending airline disaster where the brave pilot safely lands the plane full of passengers
- Group play where group narrowly escapes doom and destruction
  - – Group acts as a problem-solving team where no one is left behind in their escape from a bad storm or from pretend monsters

3. Self-care and caring for others play: Or not only am I important but so is everybody else

Examples:

- Miniature figure caregiving a young person or animal
  - – Parent or grandparent figure comforting a crying child
  - – Mama or daddy feeding the baby
  - – Families doing things together and helping each other
  - – Parent animal figure feeding their young
- Individual baby doll play or action figure play where child practices taking care of the needs of the helpless ones
  - – Mama puts her babies to bed and checks on them as they sleep
  - – An angel guards the home at night while the family sleeps
- Caregiver as model play
  - – Caregiver models how to play and care for baby dolls, and has child copy caregiving actions

4. Trust-building play: Or I can trust those who love me to supply my needs

Examples:

- Allowing someone bigger and stronger than they are to take care of them

- Miniature figure play and action figure play
    - Could be a Jedi knight rescuing the family or the children from danger
    - Could be mom or dad turning into the Jedi knight who rescues the children from danger
    - What about a child praying to God for help with some matter, and He comes and talks with them!

- Group play
    - Group meal-time play where children take turns being the mother or father who feeds the family members around the table from a play kitchen

Neuro-behavioral play which helps make courage, resiliency, and the Fruit of the Spirit easier to maintain

Instructions for many of these activities can be found on the Internet. The performance of some of these activities can be found on YouTube.

1. Vestibular system activities (strengthening the brain's air traffic controller to direct higher brain functions such as proprioception, differentiation, and interhemispheric integration)

Examples:

- Jump rope

- Body rolling activities and games
    - Slow yogic neck rolls, first to the right, then to the left
    - Knee bouncing games where children are slowly lowered backward

- Rocking in a rocking chair or swinging on a swing
- Chinese jump rope
- Blowing activities
- Ring around the Roses
- Hop scotch
- Rhythmic ball or rocking horse (especially one with springs) bouncing activities
- Real horseback riding
- Pretend horseback ride on someone's back

Note: If child's ears become red or face becomes flushed, stop activity. If child shows emotional stress of any kind, stop activity. The vestibular system has had enough exercise. Any further vestibular movement of that kind will not enhance that system but can irritate the brain. Stressed brains don't learn.

2. Proprioception activities (feeling where the body begins and ends and jarring the joints to activate the sense of self)

Examples:

- Limbo
- London Bridge
- Red Rover
- Hula hooping
- Pogo sticking
- Paddle ball play
- Blindfolded or eyes closed games
  - Pin the Tail on the Donkey
  - Smack the Pinata
  - Touch the person who is sneaking around you game
  - Blind Man's Bluff

- Potato sack races

- Human wheelbarrow races

3. Differentiation play (practicing stop/go movements, and isolation of body parts to increase impulse and emotional control)
Examples:

- Pick up sticks

- Jacks

- Yo-yo play

- Marble games

- Finger string games

    - Cup and Saucer

    - Jacob's Ladder

- Red Light, Green Light

- Musical Chairs

- Mother, May I?

- The Quiet Game

- The Hot Lava Game

- Twister®

- Operation®

- Basketball dribbling on one side of the body, then on the other

Note: Help children *prevent movement* of unnecessary body parts when playing differentiation games. For example, a child does not need to stick out his tongue to shoot marbles.

4. Interhemispheric integration play (to increase thinking skills and management of thoughts/feelings)

Examples:

- Hide and go seek games
- Skipping games
- Dancing games
  - The Hokey Pokey
  - "This A-Way Valerie (Strut Miss Suzie)"
- Cross-lateral clapping and lummi stick tapping games
- Crawling races (especially the Military Crawl) or crawling activities such as the Crab Walk
- Cross-legged walking: Walk the tight rope
- Marching to patriotic music
- The Rock, Scissors, Paper Game
- Group sports activities
  - Volleyball
  - Baseball
  - Basketball
- Simon Says
- Jumping jacks, while standing or while lying down on the floor
- Bike riding
- Any group or solitary problem-solving pretend play games that require planning, common sense, cooperation, and sequential order thinking
  - Escape from imaginary danger games
  - Rescue games
  - Treasure hunts

- – Scavenger hunts
- – Easter egg hunts
- Chinese Checkers
- Chess
- Puzzles
- Any board games which require thinking and patience

Things to consider

- Pretend play must have good endings, so resiliency, hope, and faith can be nurtured.

- If children prefer scary play with bad endings, the caregiver must help them restructure the play so good wins over evil.

- Let the children decide what the danger, emergency, or menace is in pretend play. We don't want to cause even more anxiety for them by planting something in their minds that is too scary for them.

- If any pretend play or neuro-behavioral play activities cause obvious anxiety for the child, either restructure the activity so that the child isn't frightened or let the child watch others doing it until they feel like they can try. For example, if a blindfold over the eyes causes "fight" resistance or "flight/freeze" evasion, then just have the child close his eyes and perform the activity. Another example is to let the child have the control of the movement with the vestibular system activities. Only the child can determine how much movement that system can handle.

- There is no order to the pretend play or neuro-behavioral play activities. One does not have to improve the vestibular system in order to play interhemispheric integration targeted activities. The only thing that matters is enjoyment.

CHAPTER QUESTIONS

1. What negative effects have you noticed in children due to participation in or observation of too much sedentary screen time?

2. Do your children have cell phones or other such electronic devices for play or communication? Do you set any limits with them? What are the limits?

3. How much time a day do you allow the children in your care to watch TV or play on technological devices with screens? What do they do instead?

4. Do you set limits with your children regarding Internet access? What are the rules in your home and how do you enforce them?

5. As violence in our society has increased, so have violent movies, TV programs, and computer games. Which in your opinion came first? Violence in society or violence on screens? In other words, which is the cause and which is the effect?

6. What are some pretend play and neuro-behavioral activities you remember from childhood? What were some of your pretend play themes? What were some activities that strengthened you neuro-behaviorally or helped you have more psychological or emotional resilience?

7. What are some creative play themes the children in your care enjoy? What about neuro-behavioral, physical play activities? What have you observed your children playing? What have you played with your children?

Chapter 3

Creating the Structure of the Relationship to Help Hurting Children Heal

Nurturing and nourishing the Fruit of the Spirit while courage and resiliency grow

When I was a child, one of my favorite poems was "In the Heart of a Seed" (Brown 1956, p.54). I loved it and the accompanying picture that showed the happy, healthy little seed standing on its own feet, pushing through the dirt that covered it. The seed knew where it was going, and it knew it was going to get there. All seeds rose to the sun as long as they received help. I knew that. I came from a long line of farming people. I just didn't realize at the time that I subconsciously internalized the symbolism in the poem and pictured that I was the seed, the sun was God, and the rain was the help from caregivers along my path to adulthood. The soil, however hard, represented the obstacles that would come my way. No matter what, with the proper care, I, like the seed, would be strong enough to push through the darkness and into the light.

In order for children to become like the little seed in the poem and rise up to become everything they are intended to be, caregivers must be like the rain. They must know how and when to give the nurturing and the nourishment, so that the seeds in their care can grow to healthy maturity and bear the best fruit possible.

Caregivers include all the adults who have the responsibility of raising or helping to raise children. Caregivers may be school teachers, daycare providers, babysitters, residential treatment providers, relatives, foster parents, adopted parents, step parents or birth parents. It really does take people cohesively working together in a habilitating, unified, therapeutic fashion to help a traumatized child heal.

Caregivers who have the principal responsibility of habilitating or helping hurting children to heal are ideally the home caregivers—the parents—where the child has permanent residence. Anyone who has responsibility for any child's well-being, even for a short period of time, should be acting in the highest and best interests of a child's needs and helping that child develop a healthy, loving, and giving character.

A person with a healthy character has internalized and consistently demonstrates courage, resiliency, and the Fruit of the Spirit. Childhood should be a time when children learn a healthy character from the caregivers around them—especially from the home caregivers: the family to whom they belong.

Caregiving relationships and helping a child's character grow

Parenting children is hard. Parenting hurting children is even harder. Many permanent home caregivers of traumatized children have parented their own birth children and many have not. It is common for permanent parents of these hurting children to have trouble making the "parental paradigm thinking shift" to a different type of parenting required for helping these hurting children heal, and a different kind of lens through which to see the children. In other words, what do the behaviors really mean?

Children who are hurt by someone else frequently come in to their new permanent homes without an internalized secure base of safety–security–protection and with broken or never developed trust because a caregiver with healthy character was never there for them consistently enough. So, these children, when they come into permanent living arrangements, are hardly ever calm, cool, and collected.

Birth children of healthy, mature caregivers begin growing their secure base in utero and further develop that secure base as their family continues to provide for their needs after they are born. Trust develops much more easily. Great character is much more easily developed by good parenting.

The socio-emotional and physical needs of the infant that lead to the gradual development of healthy character (like the healthy parents possess) are met naturally within the family structure as the infant grows. During the first year of life after birth, babies are held and comforted and their needs for survival, safety, and sustenance are fulfilled as necessary by attentive caregiving. Infants' safety–security–protection needs are met over and over again, so trust develops quickly: babies cry and someone they know comes and resolves their problems.

When safety–security–protection needs are met over and over again by the same caregivers, then trust naturally develops. As the child becomes more mobile, the trusting child tests the caregivers. It is important at the toddler stage that toddlers begin learning that not only are they important but so is everybody else. They frequently aren't too happy about that. The healthy caregivers model and overtly teach respect for other living creatures, which results in the child learning better behavioral boundaries and a better way to be in relationship with others.

The environment of safety–security–protection doesn't go away; it never goes away. Children must have safety, security, and protection so their brains can develop neuro-behaviorally and socio-emotionally as they should, so that good character development isn't interrupted.

As birth children in healthy families grow in safety–security and trust with the caregivers who tend to them, so does the children's attachment to their caregivers. Children begin to prefer certain caregivers to provide their needs. They know who they want to be with because that is where they can relax and feel safe, which the brain needs for good growth. When they are with those preferred caregivers, they are secure, calm, and content. The attachment to and trust for the individual caregivers grows to an attachment to the family, or village, that helps raise the child, with the preferred caregivers still central to the child's preferred well-being. In other words, these children know who they belong to. With the support, the encouragement, and the character skills learned from the family, the child can extend out into the world of others, with those same family-learned values, morals, and scruples intact as the child progresses toward adulthood.

Building the hurting child's character while helping heal the hurt

All caregivers have to work harder with hurting children. Home caregivers have to work the hardest. More attention and time need to be devoted to build the necessary base of safety–security–protection and trust. The base has to be revisited time and time again. Hurting children typically don't build trust quickly for new caregivers. Trust takes time, and it is built on the courage, protection, and consistency of the caregivers.

Many parents who bring hurting children into their home to live permanently have to make three necessary parental paradigm thinking shifts. The first shift for healing parents to really, really get is that love and a good home are never enough to build the secure base upon which character is built. For a long time, the permanent parent will be the child's primary teacher, not mother or father. The children begin to see their permanent home caregivers as their "parents" after trust and respect are built and a sense of belonging is in progress. It takes a while for children who come from hurting places to want to belong to the parents and families who are raising them. It also takes time for them to develop the self-value to believe that they are good enough for the families who want them. Many of the children are bonded to other people who may have been good to them and for them or they may have bonded with people who weren't good for them. The new parents can't force a child to commit to them. But the new parents have to commit to the children they have brought into their homes to raise.

The second parental thinking paradigm shift is that caregivers should strive to determine when a child is being a "can't" and when a child is being a "won't." Learning to recognize the brain state a hurting child is in takes observation, patience, training, and tutelage from others wiser, more trained, and more experienced.

The third parental paradigm thinking shift that permanent parents of hurting children have to make is that the growth of their child's character is sequentially in step with the resolution of past hurt and harm (see Figure 3.1). As trauma and loss resolve, character can healthily grow with the proper tutelage and support from the caregivers. The levels of growth are sequential, with overlap. (Humans are such complicated creatures.) One level builds upon the other, just like the levels of a house. Levels 1 and 2 are human needs. That's the ground floor. The human needs in these two base levels must be in place before Levels 3, 4, and 5 can healthily come on line. That way, courage, resiliency and the Fruit of the Spirit can better manifest, not just as behaviors, but as true ways of being in the world and in relationship with others.

Build Character as Hurt Resolves

(A Socio-Emotional Growth Structure for Caregivers of Hurting Children)

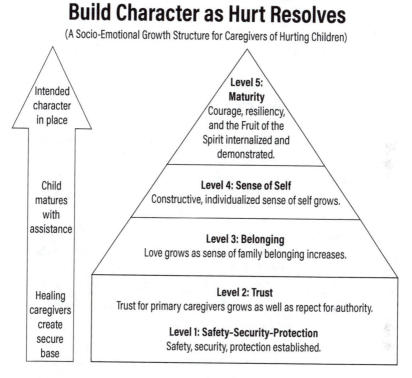

Figure 3.1 Building character as hurt resolves chart

Safety–security–protection level

This level goes beyond food, consistent nurturing, clothing, and shelter. It begins and ends with adult caregivers who are, themselves, courageous, resilient, and who have internalized the Fruit of the Spirit. Adults can't teach what they haven't learned. Non-traumatized children see every move a caregiver makes; traumatized children study every move a caregiver makes.

Beyond the infant stage, a traumatized child's initial, most important human need can be summed up in the questions,

"Will I stay here? Is this my forever home? Is this person who is physically bigger than I am strong enough to keep me safe (even if it is from myself)?" A traumatized child's sense of feeling protected from harm precedes the need for feeling loved. Protection first, then trust/respect forms so that love and belonging can come on line. Children cannot learn to trust until they begin to feel safe. Children cannot relax into receiving love, nor relax into giving love until they begin to trust and respect others.

When children relax into a sense of relative safety, then their fight–flight–freeze centers are calmed down. They don't have to spend their time figuring out ways to protect themselves and to take care of their own human needs and desires. When they begin to trust that the caregiver in charge will protect them so they don't have to protect themselves, love can find an easier way into their hearts.

Hurting children may not possess the best physical or emotional memories of adults keeping them safe. Besides consistent food, clothing, and shelter, the benevolent, consistent protection from harm by caregivers has to be well established before hurting children will begin to depend consistently on the adults who are caring for them to provide their needs. Children have to know the caregiver that they are going to trust will take a bullet for them if need be. Children don't learn to trust overwhelmed caregivers who are having their own meltdowns due to stress.

Appropriate caregiver response and action are important in the establishment of safety–security–protection for children. Children, who are predominantly "fight" when they sense threat can easily overpower an adult caregiver who is predominantly a "flight–freeze" in their response to threat. An effective, habilitating caregiver has to be more hardheaded and determined than a hardheaded, determined child. Alternatively, an adult caregiver who is predominantly a "fight" when threat is perceived must be careful not to go over the top in reaction to a "fight" or even a "flight" child in action. Temperance and training are called for so that good thinking prevails on the part of the headstrong caregiver.

Children are not going to move on to the next level, which is trust and respect for others, if they sense their caregivers aren't strong enough to protect them. Does the caregiver have the inner strength, the good thinking, the determination, the commitment, and the courage to handle the amount of stress that these hurting children can shell out without becoming like hurting children themselves? Or are the caregivers constantly reduced to fears, tears, resignation, or tantrums because of a child's behaviors? How does that get children off the fight–flight–freeze continuum so they can develop healthy character? Caregivers must work hard to identify and resolve their own issues in order to raise healthier children. Their own internal house must be strong and supported.

At the safety–security–protection level, games, caregiver–child activities, and joint play need to focus on helping the child feel safe, secure, and protected by the caregiver. This level forms the base from which resiliency is built.

Trust level

At this level, children feel safe enough to begin to relax into the comfort of a real relationship with someone and also to test the waters. This is actually when a child can relax and feel good just being next to the caregiver. The child isn't as stiff as a board next to the caregiver or alternatively clinging to the caregiver for dear life. This is when the child will risk being vulnerable with the caregiver. An example might be: a child wants to talk about what she is afraid of, what happened in the past in that hurting place that she came from, and wants the caregivers to listen and help solve the problem. Control issues become less apparent. The child can admit to having some problems.

Likewise, it doesn't always have to be the child's way because the child has learned that she won't "die" if the caregiver doesn't grant every wish or fulfill every desire. Unless, the child has obsessive compulsive disorder, which would make it hard for her to shift off of what she wants, then it's about presence or absence of trust. Children who don't trust that the caregiver will come through for them and provide for their needs, keep asking the caregiver to do so.

Children gradually begin trusting that their caregiver will come back because their caregivers are strong, consistent, and dependable. This is why it is so hard for traumatized children to experience the loss of a babysitter, or a daycare teacher, once trust starts to develop for them. This is why these children have such a hard time if their school teacher is out on extended leave due to medical reasons and a substitute teacher takes the teacher's place. This is why children who have been living in a good foster home for a long time have such a hard time adjusting to the next home caregiver, even when the setting is the permanent or forever home. With every move or with every change in caregiving, children who came from hard, hurting places find it harder to establish safety–security–protection and trust.

The development of trust and respect for others is essential for children to develop and satisfy a longing to belong. They seek to fulfill that need in the next level of socio-emotional growth.

As trust is developing, respect for others must be modeled and taught. Again, this is the level that children are being actively taught that not only are they important but so is everybody else.

It is important to teach children to put others first and to consider someone else's needs. Because the courage to do so begins at this stage, caregivers should be sowing the seeds of altruism (putting others first). The negative traits of narcissism and selfishness should be heavily discouraged at this level and at all upper levels. Children may resist being demoted from being the most important people on the face of the earth, and that's okay—they'll get over themselves.

It is important that children see courage demonstrated by caregivers as they help other people get their basic human needs met. Activities, games, and creative play should reflect sharing, demonstrating courage under fire to help others, and being a person on whom others can depend. The golden rule is emphasized in relationships, activities, and play: "Do unto others, the way you would have them do unto you."

A game that I fondly remember playing as a child with the kids in the neighborhood was "Three-Day Army." Yes, for whatever reason, we played it consecutively for three days. Playing army was important. In my day, the kids in my neighborhood had fathers who had fought in and survived World War II. Many World War II television shows were about the Allies defeating the Axis powers during that war. In the shows the soldiers were heroic and had to depend on and trust each other to defeat the enemy and survive the battles. So, we kids played what we saw on TV.

I was always the fighting nurse when we played "Three-Day Army." Okay, there never was a fighting nurse on any of the

World War II TV shows, but I thought it would have been a great continuing story line in one.

So, as the fighting nurse I always carried a machine gun (pretend, of course) and used it to protect and defend others from harm. I would have the neighborhood boys "cover" me from the enemy with their imaginary fire as I rescued babies from an orphanage. The orphanage was a mimosa tree (lots of low branches) where I carefully placed an assortment of baby dolls. I rescued as many dolls as I could each time I raced back and forth to the tree while surviving enemy fire and protecting my brood at the same time. I even stopped a time or two between rescue missions to give it back to the enemy, while yelling "You won't hurt these babies." This type of healthy play helped me develop courage, trust in others to support me, and a healthy, heroic way of being in the world and helping others...even if it meant risking my own life so others could live.

Belonging level

Healthy attachment is happening. It occurs when the longing to belong is on the way to becoming satisfied and the children in permanent care get it that they are "home," a safe and accepting place to be. When children relax into trust and respect for the caregivers, then the children can relax into love from and for the caregivers. The caregivers have survived all the trials and tribulations that the child could dish out, and proved that they were made of "the right stuff." Children can now begin to transfer the love and respect they've developed for their home caregivers out to extended family members and on to the world.

At this level, the child can sit with the caregiver and enjoy the person's smell, heartbeat, rhythm of breath, and touch. This is when the child unconsciously imitates the caregiver's vocal intonations, speech expressions, body language, and even way of walking. This is when the child bonds, admires, and attaches with the caregiver, and, in so doing, becomes like the caregiver in so many different ways.

During this time children demonstrate family loyalty, family values, and they are proud of the people to whom they belong. There is a "we" in their speech when they talk or write about things that pertain to their family. They like to hear old family stories that have been passed down. And they strive to make their home caregivers proud of them. This level, quite frankly, is when time out, as a consequence, can be quite effective because at this level children will work to get back to their attachment figures. They will strive to behave at school because they don't want their home caregivers disappointed with them.

At this level children who were adopted well after birth and have memories of the birth family may go through a period of not wanting to grow up. This is because they may want and need more time, belonging to the adopted family before they go out on their own.

Children first "belong to the tribe" before they begin to relate to their own individual selves and to the higher power that they cannot see, but who resides in the center of their being. Spiritual beliefs and practices of the family are more easily accepted and followed at the belonging level.

When a child is at the level of wanting to belong, the Fruit of the Spirit that the family demonstrates can be better internalized. The child says, "I want to be like them, and I want to be with them." Activities, games, and play should be about going home to family and belonging to a positive group that works together for the greater good, like "good guys versus bad guys with good guys winning." The play themes and activities should emphasize the Fruit of the Spirit and, as always, courage. Family mission trips, and family volunteering at nursing homes, soup kitchens, and animal shelters are well worth the effort at this level because strong families do what they can to help make the world a better place for others.

This level is about team efforts and group efforts. "All for one and one for all" like the Three Musketeers! It's about children being supported by the parents when it's time to confess a human error and then being supported to make amends to the ones they hurt by their faulty decision because being truthful, having the courage to confess, and then making amends are family values!

Sense of self level

By this level, children should be sensitive to others' needs, and should be ready to figure out how to help those in need. They can use their prior experience of hurting to feel and understand how others feel and to seek to help heal, not to help hurt like they were previously hurt. Real empathy and the courage to do something to help make someone's life better should become apparent here, because family values are internalized.

Children at this level certainly are hurting less, if at all. They are ready to practice meeting their own needs without hurting anyone else. The conscience, that little voice inside of them, which is really the internalized parent, guides them in how they treat others. When they are wrong, they may need some help promptly admitting it and making amends for their mistakes. But their overall picture looks good. Their intentions are honorable, and their behavior overall evidences that their hearts are in the right place.

Children at this level are learning who they are as individuals. They are learning how they fit into the world. They are learning to give without expecting something in return, and giving not just to make their parents happy. They should feel better about themselves when they do the right thing.

This is the level when children start earning their own self-esteem and start developing their own self-identity. They grow their own self-esteem through their works. Their positive self-identity strengthens. Their self-worth, which previously had been heavily nurtured by the caregivers, now begins to increase because of what they do and what they think with less dependency on caregiver feedback. They begin to pat themselves on the back for jobs well done—non-narcissistically, of course.

They begin to trust their own "gut" and make better moral decisions because of the internalized parent. They are less susceptible to bad influences. They are more self-aware and more self-responsible.

Play, relationships, and activities at this stage are about sharing the Fruit of the Spirit with others, which are the internalized family's values. Emphasis should be on helping to make the world a just and better place for others. Individual acts of altruism like volunteering at animal shelters, traveling on mission trips without the family, and helping residents at nursing homes without the family are wonderful activities that should be encouraged at this stage. As well, participation in activities that help children develop the natural gifts they have been given, like athleticism, musical ability, or dance, or most any innate talent should be promoted at this level.

Maturity level

By this level, parents have done all they can do to shape character and heal hurts, so children are on their own to travel through mature adulthood. They should be good thinkers, good doers, and do gooders. Mature people of excellent character should be self-honest, self-aware, self-responsible, courageous, and protective of others who are smaller and/or younger than they are. Natural components of their personality should reveal a strong sense of integrity, an ability to reason and accurately perceive reality, and an open and deep personal relationship with God.

Parents, please remember that true adulthood is not at age 18. The frontal lobes (behind the forehead) of the smart part of the brain may not be fully mature for girls until around age 25. The frontal lobes for boys may not be fully mature until about age 28. That means that there should be some minor bumps in the road to posterity until the smart part of the brain reaches its full potential.

Courage, resilience, the family values of a good family, and the Fruit of the Spirit are integral, demonstrative components of a person with excellent character. The student now has become the teacher and will be able to model and teach to others what has been learned.

More on building children's character while helping them resolve past trauma

Levels overlap

Because levels can run into each other, certain activities of different levels can be mixed. For example, a child can take gymnastics (a potential activity for the sense of self level) when the child is still learning to trust and respect the home caregiver as well as others. The child learns to trust that the caregiver will take her home after the class regardless of how well she performs and regardless of how well she behaves in class. The child might get experience in learning that if she doesn't respect the caregiver or the instructor or the other children in the class, then her disrespectful behavior will not be tolerated. Even further, she will have to make amends to those she annoyed, as well as face some type of consequence afterwards. The child also has an opportunity to begin learning that, even when the skill she's learning is physically hard, "practice makes perfect." Even if she can't do it perfectly, she learns that her caregiver is happy for her that she tried and proud that she didn't give up. She also learns that it's important to try, try again, and that not giving up is a component of that particular family's values.

The suggestions made at the end of each explanation of the various levels of character development are merely ideas. It is important that the caregivers use their thinking ability to decide when to do what because of the character lessons they wish their child to learn, and because of the individual nature of their child. The suggestions that go with the level descriptions aren't mandates for particular levels, they're just ideas.

Levels cannot be skipped

Parents who have just gotten the kids who will stay with them really shouldn't take them on a "look how much fun we are" trip to Disney World upon first arrival. Disney World isn't the real world; life in a family isn't all fun. New parents don't want to set up the brand new children who have come to live with them to think of them as cash cows.

An initial arrival all-expenses-paid trip to La-La Land is setting a template for the child's character development within the family, all right: it's called narcissism and "gimme-gimme." With an initial arrival, caregivers should focus on safety and security rules where the parents are benevolently in charge and children are not being waited on. So much of the safety–security–protection level is about setting the template for what the family's character is about, which the children will adopt because they will become like the family who raises them. What follows is a true example of that.

Years ago when I was a newly minted psychotherapist, one of my favorite mentors told me how, in her childhood, she had come to live with her permanent family. My mentor had been raised in an orphanage in the United States until she was six years old. The family who adopted her were honest, hardworking "salt of the earth" type folks who owned a general store and ran together as a family. My mentor told me how, on day one of living with the family, her parents put her to work in the store, alongside them, starting her off on a very "important job." She didn't realize it at the time, but on the first day when she went home to live with them the family started teaching her their values, which led to the development of her present outstanding adult character.

She said the family got her up early in the morning and took her to their store with them. The first thing her adopted mother did was show her how to organize and line up the cans of English peas on the store shelf. Her mom worked on another shelf beside her.

Relaying this story, my mentor's eyes gleamed with pride as she remembered that experience from so long ago. She told me that was the first time anyone thought she had the ability to accomplish anything. She was so happy with herself that she could do something and that her new family really was pleased with her work.

It made her happy that she really could help the family who had helped her by taking her in. She also said that she just knew they wouldn't send her back to the orphanage because they needed her to help them. As we all do, she needed to be needed.

Day by day, as safety–security–protection grew and trust and respect for the family who was raising her formed, she grew incrementally in love and belonging to them as they did to her.

When I knew her, she was in her seventies and still working hard to help make the world a better place. She was an early, well-known, well-respected psychotherapist in the field of trauma-focused care, or trauma resolution as it was called in that day. She was a beautiful, courageous, resilient, altruistic human being, through and through.

Just as no two fingerprints are alike, no two children are alike

Children must be understood as having individual needs. Some children take longer to progress to the upper rungs of the house of character and trauma resolution (as depicted in Figure 3.1) than other children do. These children need more time, parent attention, and professional help to be able to do so. Multiple factors determine their speed of resiliency.

Certainly, the more hurting children a family takes into their home, the more primary, permanent habilitating caregivers need to be on hand to help. The story of the "Little Old Woman Who Lived in a Shoe," *who had so many children she didn't know what to do*, was a quite fitting poem for the adoptive mom who gave

Maribel (the child on "flight" continuum from Chapter 1) and siblings a permanent home. Mom was too overwhelmed with the needs of the collective group of hurting children in her care. Due to this fact, she was unable to personally deliver all that an individual hurting child needed to develop character and to heal the past trauma and losses that were preventing the child from joining the permanent family in body, heart, mind, and spirit.

Maribel, as the reader will remember, was the oldest female of a large adopted group of siblings. She was the child who just couldn't step up to the plate and be Mom's little helper. She came into the family that adopted her as a shy, frightened, four-year-old little girl who had bonded with her birth mother, but who never bonded with her adopted mother, nor very deeply with her birth siblings.

Maribel had been the birth mother's little helper with the numerous back-to-back children that she gave birth to until the state came in and removed the children due to the birth mother's inability to properly care for them. Maribel is an adult now and hasn't so far developed the character of the family who adopted her like her siblings did. She also hasn't sufficiently resolved the old hurts and fears that negatively impacted her socio-emotional growth as a young child.

Maribel never did develop trust with the mother who adopted her. She stayed stuck at Level 2 of the first floor of the Building Character and Resolving Hurt House. She never reached Level 3, that sense of belonging and love for the primary caregivers in her family. As a result, she never got to herself and created a constructive, individualized, complete human being who acts it as well. Presently, she's on her own, a lost child in an adult's body. Although she has internalized some of the Fruits of the Spirit, she lacks many important traits, including the courage to protect her young ones when they come, the altruism to provide for their needs, and the maturity to instill excellent character in them. Her children may be the ones taking care of her, when they are far too young to be doing so.

Recovery from loss, hurt, and harm is a sequential, slow process with ups and downs and setbacks along the way

Recovery looks like this:

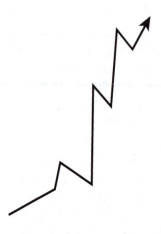

Not like this:

Many children from hurting places take two or three steps forward and one step back. Change is incremental with small setbacks along the way, and that's okay. That's normal. It's supposed to take a while and a lot of work for new ways of thinking and being to become permanent and life changing. It's important that caregivers never lose hope, never stop praying, never stop looking for answers, and never stop seeking support for themselves so they can continue to be their children's greatest teachers of hope and healing.

CHAPTER QUESTIONS

1. A couple has a new foster-to-adopt child in their home. He has been there a month. So, far he is doing well behaviorally and they have no complaints at this time. They want to bring him to a counselor who does individual therapy with children as soon as possible, so he can have his own therapist in case he wants to keep things confidential from the adopting parents. He is nine years old. They also want him to get a jump start on resolving the hurt and harm he has experienced, so they want to start therapy before he has any problems. Refer to Figure 3.1 and the accompanying descriptions. How many potential problems do you see with the adopting parents' line of thinking?

2. It is hard for people to change. The older people get, the harder it is, but it is not impossible. Parental paradigm thinking shifts are very hard to change if parents have raised their own birth children successfully and have adopted troubled children for whom the same parenting techniques just don't work. How have you, as parents of hurting children, been challenged in developing a new parenting paradigm?

3. How do you seek support from others to help you "refill your well" so you can have more water to give to the children in your care?

4. Ponder this statement, please: "Love isn't a feeling; it's a commitment." What does this mean to you?

Chapter 4

Build the Foundation for Mature Character through Safety–Security-Protection-Trust Actvities and Experiences

Bye-Bye Baby Bunting.
Daddy's gone a hunting.
To catch a little rabbit skin,
To wrap his Baby Bunting in.

Mother Goose

When I was a small child being cared for by my aunt, she sang this song while rocking me to a slow 60-beat-a-minute rhythm. My aunt took over my care when my mother's mental illness made it unsafe for my sister and me to be with her. What a contrast in care. My aunt's rhythm, voice, words, touch, and smell were so much more soothing than my mother's. With my aunt, I could relax. I didn't have to struggle to get away or dissociate into a floppy, non-moving, barely breathing, pretending-to-be-dead little girl. My aunt exuded safety and calm that soothed my restlessness.

Resting against my aunt's chest, I felt the slow, consistent beat of her heart. I relaxed into the protection of her arms wrapped gently around me. Her voice, vibrating from her chest into my ears, awakened the proprioceptive neural impulses in my face that told me where I was in time and in space. Grounding me with her body, she held me so I wouldn't fall. Wrapped in her loving arms, I felt safe enough to close my eyes. The sweet smell of my aunt's skin pleasured the lower, emotional center of my brain, enticing me to lie close and be still just a little bit longer. The more my caregiver sang and rocked me, the more her song and her rhythm calmed and relaxed her. As she calmed and relaxed, so did I. We shared a pleasurable experience. We connected in a happy, healing way.

My receptive language was developing. Her words and touch assured me that there was someone much bigger and stronger than I was who had my best interests at heart. She was unafraid and confident in her ability to nurture. She put me first. By her loving actions, she was forming a template in my brain of safety–security–protection–trust in a higher power through a concrete, much-bigger-than-myself human being. The safety and security I felt in her arms paved the way for my future belief and faith in a loving, abstract, not-of-this-earth higher power.

Adults create healthy, secure attachment in children through positive "real" non-virtual, physical interaction with them. Caregivers are able to instill in children safety–security–protection–trust because loving, protective adults instilled it in them. Caregivers who haven't themselves experienced dependable, protective others can't teach what they don't know to the children who rely on them to meet their socio-emotional needs. My birth mother couldn't. But my aunt and uncle, my grandma, and my first-grade teacher, Miss Beetles, could. They were the human caregiving angels God sent my way. Thus, in spite of the hard beginnings I had, the template was established, in childhood, for the "me" I am today because of caregivers like them who somehow understood what I needed and were able to provide it.

Internalized safety–security–protection–trust is the base from which self-esteem, self-confidence, self-responsibility, self-strength, and altruism develop. It is the support upon which mature character or the internalized Fruit of the Spirit must build. Without an internalized secure base, children develop anxiety and self-deception. When a child has a secure base in childhood with positive attachment to a preferred, stable, protective, and physically present primary caregiver, then a healthy relationship with God, whom we cannot see, is much easier.

Insecurely attached and developmentally traumatized children often succumb to unhealthy control, anxiety, mistrust of those who love them, and abusive behaviors. As adults they either become their own God (unhealthy narcissism) or they may find God in substances or toxic behaviors. Reversing unhealthy belief systems is difficult but not impossible. It's work that is definitely not for the faint of heart, nor for parents who take a child's antics personally, as if it is "them" whom the child is out to get by interpreting their "can'ts" as "won'ts."

Therapeutic caregivers of children who hurt seek the sources of the unpleasant symptoms that they see, and they address those sources from a psychological, neuro-behavioral, socio-emotional and spiritual growth perspective. A child's ability to trust in an adult caregiver to protect them trumps any other socio-emotional need in childhood. This is the base upon which the quality of the relationship with self, with others, and with God is built. A child who has experienced significant neglect, abuse, loss, and chronic and acute stress has an even greater need for safety and security experiences with loving, mature, and stable adults. They have a harder time developing trust because it has been broken, sometimes again and again.

Below are some therapeutic activities, attitudes, and experiences that parents can share and enjoy with the children in their care to help them establish an essential base of safety–security–protection–trust.

Caregiver-child rocking chair time to help calm brain and body

Caregivers can rock with children to help them transition from an alert to a drowsy brain state. This comforting act helps regulate them when they are fretting and need help regulating themselves. It also provides parent–child quality "love and bonding" time.

How comforting rocking feels for both parties involved. Caregivers can even rock themselves when they feel out of sorts. Rocking helps soothe and calm the brain, and establishes a rhythm that the cerebellum (perhaps the brain's motherboard) needs. Even older children can be rocked; it's not just for infants and toddlers.

Caregivers should add a slowly sung comforting song, hum something spiritually soothing, or just gently make a "shush" sound with their lips and tongue while taking slow, long, and deep breaths. A regulated parent helps regulate a child. The drawn out "shush" sound and the slow, rhythmic rocking replicates the sound and the movement the gestational infant at least should have received in utero. This movement and sound helps the baby's lower brain develop in a healthier way to better manage stress.

Caregiver-initiated knee-bouncing games to help install rhythmic synchronicity and nurture trust in children

One of my favorite close times with the adults who loved and enjoyed me as a child was to "Go See Mr. Brown." I'm not sure where this knee-bouncing game originated, but it could have been passed down generationally through my South Mississippi maternal ancestors.

To perform this adult-activated activity, the child first sits, facing the adult, on the adult's knees. It's important that the adult's face and body language convey confidence and fun with lots of facial expression and eye contact. The adult securely holds onto the child while the child securely holds onto the adult. Then the adult bounces the child slowly and consistently up and down on the knees in synchrony with the words and the 60-beat-a-minute rhythm of the following song:

Mr. Brown went to town

Riding a goat and leading a hound.

The hound barked; the goat jumped.

Threw Mr. Brown right down on a stump!

Surprise! The child does not tumble onto the floor. Instead, the adult gently, slowly, and securely tilts the child backward as far as the child can comfortably tolerate without showing signs of anxiety and fear. Then slowly, the adult returns the child to a sitting position on top of the knees. The adult then asks the child, "Who kept you from falling on that stump?"

"You did!" is the desired answer.

"And I will every time!" can be the adult response.

As the child grows in trust that the adult performing the activity will keep him safe from falling, and will stop if the activity scares him, then the adult may gradually increase the speed at which the child is tilted. In the situation of a hyper-vestibular child (child fearful of too much movement), that may not be by much because the part of the brain which reads and adjusts to movement isn't working as efficiently as it should.

Caregiver "large and in charge" attitude in psycho-dramatic play to help children feel safe during sleep time

Sleep time can be a frightening time for so many children. They may have trouble going to sleep and staying asleep because they are afraid. This time may have been when they were molested, or perhaps it was the time when they awoke to what other people were doing to each other that let them know that the world in which they lived wasn't safe. Also, if they were the children who had to be in control during the day to make sure that others were safe, they learned that if they were asleep, they couldn't do so. I've even had some children tell me that, if they go to sleep, the caregivers whom they are beginning to trust could die or disappear. These kids can be reminded, though play, that the adult caregiver, their real parent, is there to keep them safe when they sleep and won't disappear on them, or go away.

Here is a play activity that you should repeat to help children experience feelings of safety–security–protection–trust instead of fear during sleep time hours. This activity reminds children that the parent is ever watching over them and keeping them safe while they rest, so that they don't have to.

The parent can have the child (or children) go and lie down wherever it may be that they are having trouble resting. That may be their bed, a pallet, or some other place of rest to which they are accustomed. The caregiver sits in a chair at the door where the child or children can see them. The caregiver dims the lighting, folds her arms and acts as a guard, confidently scanning the horizon for danger. Every time I've tried this activity in a caregiver–child therapy session, a child will either pretend to awaken and cry to see if and how the caregiver will provide the rescue, or cry out that a monster or bad guy or some other threat is either in the room or trying to get in to the room. With karate hacks and kung fu kicks, or sometimes with a broom or fly swatter, the parent can chase the imaginary intruder away to the happy laughter of the children and then return to the guard post.

Practice makes perfect as the old saying goes, and creating a new way of being in the world and with others takes time, effort, and lots of repetition. The more fun the practice is, the better the brain retains the new information. The more physical the practice is, the better the body retains the memory. Humans were wired for connection to others. The more people connect in real time, real space, instead of through virtual means, the easier connecting to "real" people becomes.

A caregiver "large and in charge" attitude during crisis or emergency situations

I remember a story, whether actual or not, of the attitudes of shelter captains in London during the World War II Nazi bombing of that city. As I was told, the children were less traumatized in the shelters where the captains took charge, acted bravely and without noticeable fear regardless of what was happening outside of the shelter. The children looked to the adults in charge for their own well-being. The children in the shelters where the captains were confused and visibly frightened suffered more symptoms of post-traumatic stress disorder. The confidence level of the adults in charge made the difference in the children's mental health.

This story made sense to me. If caregiving adults aren't in control of crisis situations, then children have to be, and they don't know how. The story also helps me understand why we need heroes. Heroes keep us safe. They do for us and for others what we can't do for ourselves.

My aunt was one of my heroes. I experienced on more than one occasion how her fast-acting courage in crisis situations saved children from certain danger. Her actions to protect children proved she was big enough to protect me if I needed it.

I remember visiting an old Spanish fort with a group of other tourists of varying ages. I must have been about five or six years old. We came upon a section of the fort that had a steep, stone stairwell with no guard rails which led to a second floor. It was dark and creepy with no lighting. People who explored those stairs had to place their hands along the walls of the stairwell and feel their way up, or down. The sign before the stairwell, I was later told, said, "Enter at Your Own Risk."

Suddenly, a frantic father emerged from the stairwell carrying a bleeding, screaming child and raced toward the exit. I knew the child had fallen. He shouted to his other children, who were somewhere in that dark passageway, to stay where they were and he would come back for them. The terrified children pleaded, over and over again at the top of their lungs, "Don't leave us! Somebody, please help us!" Even I knew they could try to follow their father and tumble down the stone steps like their sibling had done.

I scanned the adults in our little tour group. No one moved. They just stared at the stairwell, frozen in time and space, not reacting. They were supposed to do something, say something. I wanted to but knew I was too little. I felt helpless.

All of sudden, my precious aunt, in a time when women weren't supposed to be heroes, pushed past all the non-reacting adults in our group and sped toward the darkened stairwell. She shouted to the children in her biggest voice that she was coming to get them and that they weren't to move. Their cries stopped, and they obeyed.

She was strong; she was sure. One by one, she brought each stranded, terrified child safely down the stairs, assuring them that she wouldn't let them go. She directed the ones still waiting to be led down to stay calm and wait, that they would be okay until she could get to them. They obeyed her. They believed her. They waited their turn to be escorted down. They trusted her, a strange woman they had never met and couldn't see. But they must have felt God's strength through her hands, her feet, her breath, her voice, and her bravery. No other adults volunteered to step forward and assist her.

I knew then my aunt could and would move mountains to keep me safe. And I could let her. She didn't think of her own safety. She only thought of the children who needed her. Years later, my aunt confided that she felt a force much greater than herself propelling her body up and down those stairs and speaking the words from her mouth during that event. She would take no credit for it herself.

A caregiver has to be a traumatized child's hero. If caregivers have to work on themselves to develop courage, then they should do so. Real courage comes from a faith in and a dependence on a benevolent power much greater than self. Traumatized children need to know their caregiver is strong and brave enough to protect them, not through words, but though action. Experience speaks louder than words.

Caregivers helping children structure play with miniature figures to practice the concept of safety and protection by others

Some children are emotionally healthy enough to perform their own play therapy with miniature figures without adult guidance and intervention. In my practice, I've had some traumatized children who were and some who weren't.

I remember the little boy who kept putting Jesus in the closet of the toy house he was playing with. I asked him why and he told me that he had to protect Jesus because the burglars were coming. If the child had to protect Jesus, then who was going to protect him? So, his adopted mom and I helped transform the Jesus miniature into…Ninja Jesus! We had the little boy instead practice, through repetitive play, Jesus keeping him and the family safe from any and all forms of destruction he could dream up. While Jesus was keeping the house safe, the pretend family, including the little boy's miniature, were sleeping safely and soundly in their beds.

Miniature figures are hard to find nowadays. It may be possible to find a few farm animals, dinosaurs, and army men in the toy section of dollar stores or at garage sales. They have fallen out of demand because children don't do a lot of imaginative three-dimensional, non-electronic or non-battery-powered play anymore unless they're getting play therapy with a professional.

When I was a child, I played with miniature figures, sometimes for hours. Although I didn't know it at the time, I was healthy enough emotionally to structure my own play based on themes of safety–security–protection–trust in others greater than myself. I just knew that I felt better after I played. When I was with my unstable birth mother, my play with miniatures reflected themes of safety–security–protection–trust. Because I didn't have safety–security–protection–trust in my home, I created it in play. That kind of play helped me be as resilient as I am today, helped form the template of safety–security–protection–trust that's made me as courageous as I am today, and gave me the hope that there was some goodness in the world. Through my own pretend play with miniatures, I was positively structuring the life I wanted to experience in the care of adults. I was never alone or frightened in my play, and I never had to take care of myself. Trustworthy adults were there to do it all for me.

One of my favorite safety–security–trust play themes with miniature figures was about the "saving of Sally." Sally was a young cowgirl on horseback (me, of course) who lived with her grandfather and his two cowboy employees on a large ranch. Any time a storm would blow up, or outlaws would come, or lions and tigers and bears would attack, the grandfather and the two cowpokes would protect Sally and all the farm animals from harm. Sally never had to worry. The problem-solving and the acts of bravery were initiated and carried out by others greater than her. Sometimes, in play, the adults in the pretend drama would rescue Sally before she had a chance to know that something was wrong. Sometimes, she was the one to run to them because she had seen trouble coming. They always took care of it, whatever it was. Sally never had to do so.

When children need help in making their play with miniatures constructive, adults have to get involved. If a child is creating a trauma drama with death, doom, and destruction, and their young hero or heroine is the only one who can keep people safe, or even dies trying, then adult caregivers need to turn the play around to make a positive outcome. It's always best to have the children pick the figures to represent themselves and the ones to represent the bad guys. The caregiving adults should select the miniatures to represent themselves, and of course they should gravitate toward strong, benevolent characters. Repetitively, in play, the caregivers need to come to the rescue and never lose to the enemy.

How does play like this help? The mind comes to believe what the body experiences, even it is through play. The more children play security and protection by trustworthy caregivers, the easier it is for them to create a sense of safety within and develop a faith in something larger than themselves.

Caregivers remaining large and benevolently in charge in spite of children who seemingly fight them for dominance

Children who fight for control in relationships are frightened and insecure. If they can control others, they think it will make them feel safer and more secure. Unfortunately, their takeovers and successful coups with the caregivers in their lives result in more insecurity and more need for control.

Children who seek to dominate the caregiver and reduce them to tears or to fearful, angry withdrawal really don't know what they are doing. A caregiver makes a mistake in thinking that they do.

"My child hates me!" I've heard so many parents say.

No, in many cases, the children want the caregivers to prove they are stronger than the children themselves are, so the children don't have to be the ones who have to protect everybody. Sometimes traumatized children battle for control of the caregivers, so the caregivers will get fed up with them and get rid of them. These children believe they are bad, so they act bad in order to get people to agree with them. Also, since they assume the caregiver will get rid of them anyway, like everyone else has, they may as well blow it up first, so they won't be surprised and further hurt when it happens.

The 1962 version of *The Miracle Worker* is a good movie for parents of hard-headed, feisty, traumatized children to see. The movie depicts how a stubborn and feisty teacher changed the life of a stubborn and equally feisty deaf, dumb, and blind child named Helen Keller by being more stubborn and determined than Helen was. Caregivers have to benevolently out-hard-head the hard-headed children in their care.

The Miracle Worker is a must-see for any parent of a difficult child who will seemingly fight to the finish for dominance. The teacher in the movie challenged the parents to stop spoiling and pitying Helen. The teacher let the parents know that the child would not begin to learn until her behavior was under control. How right she was. A hurt child does not begin to trust benevolent caregivers until safety–security–protection–trust has been established. This secure base is established when the caregivers, not the child, are in control and running the house (or the classroom). Pitying a child is one of the worst things a person can do. Pity kills. Pity enables children to be the worst they can be. It helps them be victims who victimize others instead of the resilient victors God intended them to be. If I had been pitied and enabled in my childhood, I wonder if I would be alive now. I'm afraid if I had been pitied and enabled, then I would be miserably unhappy now (if still alive) because all the unhappiness I had caused myself in my life would have been someone else's fault.

Because there were caregivers who accepted me, protected me, and were in a relationship with me even when I couldn't stand myself, and acted like it as well, I gradually learned to trust those who could be trusted and delete the need for control just for control's sake. Because I lived in an era when "real" play and "live" relationships were all we had, my brain and mind could be helped to habilitate through natural "real-world" interactions. And they did.

CHAPTER QUESTIONS

1. What are some games and activities you remember from your childhood that made you feel safe, comforted, and calm?

2. Who were the people who made you feel safe when you were young? Why? Relate some things from your memory.

3. Who were the people who didn't make you feel safe? Why?

4. What were some of the acts of heroism you witnessed when you were young or were at least aware of that made lasting impressions on you? Describe those impressions.

5. What are some activities from this chapter you could practice with the children in your care? Why and how could they be beneficial?

6. What are some experiences and activities you now create for the children in your care that helps them feel safer and more secure?

Chapter 5

Build Awareness of Self and Others through Proprioception Activities and Rhythmic Interactions

Practice makes perfect

"Boogers in the Hall"[1]

This creative "escape from danger" children's game, which also sharpened neuro-behavioral strengths such as the sense of proprioception, was played in someone's home, in the hallway. It required a designated "booger," and at least three children to escape from the booger by passing him in a dark hallway and reach safety at the hallway's end.

Because light from other rooms kept the hallway from being completely dark, the "booger" would have to wear a blindfold. His objective: to listen as the escapees slithered past him in the hall and grab them, one by one, to put them out of the game.

Sneaking carefully past the booger, the escapees had to rely upon their stealth, intelligence, physical coordination, and their cause–effect thinking (all neuro-behavioral functions) to reach safety. Passing the booger required intuitively measuring where they were going to need to be in time and in space (proprioception) to avoid contact with the booger and with the other escapees. Each time they played, escapees fine-tuned their sense of proprioception

---

1   Boogers /bʊˈgərz/ (International Phonetic Alphabet or IPA spelling); the word essentially means "monsters" or Boogie Men or Bogeymen. Long ago, "Boogers" was a common term, at least in the southeastern United States.

(see Chapter 2) which also involved hearing and kinesthesia (muscle memory).

Without his sense of sight, the booger had to rely on his sense of body in space and on hearing to detect the location and movement of the others. Giggles, heavy breathing, the squeaking of bare feet on the floor or of hands on the hallway walls were dead giveaways as to the location of the escapees.

Escapees had to practice non-verbal means to silently signal other escapees to "go," in a coordinated, timed fashion, when the game began. Elsewise, the escapees would pile up at the start and the booger could grab them all.

In this game, all players needed sharp attention and focus. Throughout, players had to be in an aroused, yet controlled (smart part of brain still in charge) alert state. Because the objective was for all the escapees to make it safely to the end of the hall, they had to work as a team. Thus, the escapees practiced keeping their wits about them as they figured out how to evade danger en masse.

Playing this game repetitively gave children's brains and bodies constructive ways to escape from real danger. In my own childhood, it helped me practice being very still, quiet, constructively alert (not careening down the fight–flight–freeze continuums), and focused. I needed those skills when hiding behind the utility room door as my birth mother, who had lost touch with reality, looked for me, ranting that I was possessed by the devil and must meet with God's justice for my sins.

I could stand there behind that door, out of sight, barely breathing, making neither move nor sound, even when my birth mother stood just a few feet from me—too close for comfort. Although I couldn't see her, I could hear her movement, her breath, her nonsensical verbal tirade. Like sonar, my hearing, which fed my sense of proprioception, helped me register approximate location of the threat due to my brain's interpretation of sound waves. Thanks to my improved sense of proprioception, I could sense how close or how far she was from me. It seemed like hours that I would stand behind that door, listening for the sound of my father's car pulling into the driveway and hearing his car door open and close. That was my signal that my world might be safer again, and I could come out from hiding.

The long hard road to self-awareness for a traumatized child

"How about some breakfast foods for our evening meal?" The stepmom asked her nine-year-old stepdaughter as she served the girl a plate of ham, eggs, and toast for the evening meal.

With a serious expression, the girl responded, "It's *not* evening. It's morning."

Dad and stepmom thought she was making a joke. They quickly realized she wasn't. The little girl thought it was morning because she had been given breakfast foods. She didn't know what time of day it was. Her memory of the events of her day hadn't tipped her off that she had already eaten breakfast and lunch.

"Don't you remember what you had for lunch today, and what you ate for breakfast this morning?"

Her wide eyes looked up to the right and then to the left as she combed both brain hemispheres for the answer. She didn't have one. Her response also indicated that she hadn't even registered environmental facts such as the waning sun beginning to cast evening shadows, the birds settling in the trees to roost, dad home from work, and the evening news broadcasting from the television set. She wasn't using memory nor the environmental details that, if nothing else, would indicate the approximate time of day for most people.

The girl had concocted a faulty system to let her know where she was in time: what kind of food she was served for a meal. When her stepmother shattered that system by serving breakfast in the evening, the girl flew into a state of anxiety and disbelief that she was willing to defend and debate, as if her sanity depended on it (and maybe it did). It had to be morning. Breakfast was served.

This child's particular primary caregiver had been her mentally ill birth mother for the early, most formative years of her life. Dad had gotten custody of her sometime later and stepmom came on board to help him with the child rearing. The girl had some major quirks in various neuro-behavioral areas such as proprioception (brain's innate knowledge of where the body is in time and in space), and interhemispheric integration (cause–effect or common sense thinking).

Her significant proprioceptive deficiency led to her confusion about time of day. With interhemispheric integration significantly delayed, she put the wrong clues together to determine time of day. The child had suffered significant neglect for two years with her birth mother. She had rarely been picked up or given attention. She spent most of her time sedentary and ignored. The proprioceptive receptors throughout her body, primarily in the joints and other connecting tissues, hadn't given her brain the information she needed to orient her in time and space. Infants need another human body to hold them enough so that the other human's movement and touch can help proprioception develop.

Infants are supposed to begin to feel and sense where they are in time and space. They figure out where they end and another begins by being moved, cuddled, coddled, and "worn" by another human. They also begin to sense and to feel a rhythm to their own bodies and to others by the timely attendance of those who consistently provide for their needs.

Nurturing caregivers repeatedly attend to crying babies to give them what they need when they need it. Rhythmically they rock and hold and comfort and pat them. They hum and speak in soft, melodic, nurturing voices. As babies are held and loved, their brains and bonds develop.

Historically, think of how some Native American mothers swaddled and carried babies on their backs as "papooses" as they went about the rhythm of their day. Mayan Indians in Central America put their babies on their backs after they were born. Mothers' consistent, rhythmic movement further developed the infants' vestibular systems (brain's superhighway), cerebellums (perhaps the brain's motherboard), and sense of proprioception.

So, the girl who had breakfast for supper—who didn't know *where* she was or *when* she was, certainly had no idea of *who* she was. Where there is a significant deficit in proprioception, there cannot be any sense of self, or for that matter, sense of another. Only after a child develops an adequate degree of proprioception to support effective common-sense thinking, can the child really start putting two and two together to make good sense and good decisions.

Without an effective sense of proprioception, one can never progress upward out of the need for safety–security and protection from others toward successful, mature adulthood. Children never leave the foundation of the house that provides support for the higher levels of human maturation (Figure 3.2, Chapter 3). The individual never becomes a successful, independent adult who can provide a safe, secure protective environment for those smaller, younger little human beings who need someone wiser and stronger than themselves to keep them safe.

Sleep time difficulties: Proprioception problems

Eight-year-old Benjamin wanted bright lights on in his room to go to sleep. Then, while sleeping, he flipped and flopped under tons of heavy covers, talked, and even walked in his sleep. It wasn't uncommon for him to sleep with his eyes partially open. At an early age Benjamin suffered neglect and abuse from his birth mother who regularly ingested any drug she could get her hands on, even when pregnant with him. After the state removed the birth family's parenting/custodial rights, a family adopted Benjamin.

Because his sense of proprioception was weak, he overused his eyes to tell him where he was in time and space. With the lights out and his eyes closed, he felt "floaty." That feeling caused anxiety because his body didn't feel grounded and his brain lost track of where he was.

Most people have had sleep time dreams (or maybe nightmares) which relate more to the past than the present. Sometimes, when waking from such dreams, people turn on the light to help orient them in time and space. They need to study their surroundings visually to gather clues as to where they are, and when they are (like how old?). People who have had these nocturnal dream world experiences may understand how scary other people can feel when they are confused about where they are in time and space.

To compensate for his proprioceptive deficit, Benjamin requested lights on, kept his eyes partially open so he could always see where he was (not great for deep, restful sleep), and used heavy covers to weigh him down. His proprioceptive deficit made it difficult for his brain to keep his body in place as he slept. As a result, he moved constantly, and sleepwalked so much that his family had to get an alarm on the outer doors of their home to keep him indoors during his dream-induced adventures. They first discovered Benjamin's nocturnal wanderings when they were woken by their outside dogs barking at Benjamin in the yard when he should have been in his bed sleeping. To their bewilderment, his parents discovered that, even while walking outside, he was sleeping.

Below are some immediate compensatory interventions that the parents instated with Benjamin (besides the house alarm) so that he could get a safer night's sleep, and they could get a less stressful night's sleep. The compensatory interventions (efforts to temporarily slow down the problem) were put in place until habilitative measures (a custom-designed professionally created program to mend brain and heal heart) could have a noticeable effect. The below bedtime interventions may help children with proprioceptive deficits or at least suspected proprioceptive deficits.

Ideas for helping children with proprioceptive deficits sleep better

Position and height of child's bed

Let the child sleep as close to the floor and as close to a wall (on at least one lengthwise side of the bed) as possible. Floors are grounding; so are walls that they can touch. It is easier for a child to feel the thumps, bumps, and security of a floor, especially a wooden floor, under a short-legged bed. During sleep, children with proprioceptive deficits may flip and flop like a just caught fish so they can feel the subtle jarring of their joints. Unfortunately, flipping and flopping is often accompanied by kicking, which means these children usually don't make very good bed partners for other children or pets.

Children with proprioceptive deficits shouldn't sleep on the top bunk, either. The higher the bed, the more insecure an already insecure body-in-space kid becomes when he attempts to rest in it. Railings may prevent these children from toppling off the side of the bed during their flipping and flopping, but why court disaster? The brain stands a chance of feeling more secure the closer the body is to the floor.

It is important for children with proprioceptive deficits to have at least one side of their bed against a wall. They may flip and flop less as their bodies may not have as much of a need to joint-jar by aggressive movement throughout the night. With the head of the bed touching one wall and one side of their bed touching another, children can touch the side wall with their hands or feet. They may even wish to sleep with their backs touching the same wall, as the wall should offer them some physical feedback of where they are. Against a wall, children may not feel so floaty and may flip and flop less.

When a child turns in a bed that has a headboard touching a wall, the action may create a jarring vibration that courses through the child's body. This vibration can feed necessary locating information to the brain through the body's connective tissues.

Insulating materials around the body

Pillows and stuffed animals pressed against the body insulate and provide proprioceptive feedback to the brain. And, yes, heavy comforters are a great idea to keep sleeping children from feeling as if they're floating away. Why, in so many cultures, are children tucked in at night? The body likes the physical security.

To help children with proprioceptive deficits, you might let them sleep with a forgiving family dog. Retrievers can be great. They're big and have tremendous patience. When children can feel another warm, living, breathing body in bed with them, animal or human, they are more secure in time and space. For the traumatized child, a big, loving, patient dog in bed with them, or on the floor close enough to touch, can prove helpful in the sleep time hours. This can aid a child's socio-emotional growth and help resolve trauma because the dog is helping provide a sense of safety–security–protection. When sleep time is safer, rest is easier.

Lighting factors

A light isn't the most helpful for deep sleep. But a child with a proprioceptive deficit in combination with a traumatic background probably needs some light. The light helps the child know where he or she is in time and space and it gives the child some sense of defense against what can go bump in the night in total darkness.

The brain gets more rest with soothing, muted colors such as soft blues, golds, or greens. Colored lights still provide some light for those with proprioceptive deficits, but not enough to trick the brain into thinking it's daylight. The lights should be solid, not blinking nor revolving. Light that moves makes it difficult for children to relax, so that they can change their brain states from wakefulness to sleepiness.

A bed tent

Some parents allow children to sleep in small tents on their bedroom floor so they feel safer and proprioceptively more secure. Instead of a real tent, parents may create a tent of blankets supported by furniture to provide the same feeling of boundaries and safety. Some companies make tents that attach to children's beds.

Inputting rhythm and beat

Therapeutic rhythm and beat change the brain. Sleep time is a good time to input subtle slow and consistent rhythm and beat to help habilitate the brain. Dr. Bruce Perry, noted child psychiatrist and senior fellow of the Child Trauma Academy in Houston, Texas stresses the healing power of rhythm and beat (Perry 2006). He advocates that slower, repetitive, consistent rhythms of 80 beats a minute can help relax and re-pattern the lower survival parts of a child's brain (the non-smart part of the brain where the states of hyper-vigilance and hyper-arousal originate).

Dr. Perry considers the optimal resting heartbeat of a pregnant mother should be about 80 beats per minute. Stress increases heartrate. Pregnant mothers with chronic stress and chronic hyper-arousal likely don't have consistent, slower heartbeats that optimally feed and healthily develop the lower survival parts of the brains of their unborn children. These children can show signs of anxiety and hyper-arousal after birth. Their brains have been prepared to be anxious.

An unborn child's chronic anxiety can cause important neuro-behavioral functions to be delayed. Their pulses may be erratic, dysrhythmic, or just too fast too often. Some of these children are misdiagnosed with ADHD, but they really have chronic anxiety. Because sleep hours may be an optimal time to help rehabilitate the brain's arousal, survival centers, creating a soothing sleep environment may help children wake feeling calmer, or at least become calmer over time.

Figure 5.1 The cuckoo clock

Even when I was a young child feeling safe with my aunt and uncle, they struggled to get me still for bed. My brain state was accustomed to being on hyper-alert and wanted to stay there. They tried room after room and bed after bed to find the best place to get me to settle down. Finally, they let me choose where I wanted to sleep. I chose the room with a cuckoo clock (Figure 5.1).

They had disabled the "cuckoo" that would wake me, leaving only the tick-tock of the clock pendulum, which slowly and consistently (60 beats a minute) rocked back and forth all night long. I would wake in the morning rested, moving slower and more rhythmically in sync with others. Not so hyper-active, I was generally more pleasant and fun to be around.

All through the night, the slow, rhythmic tick-tock relaxed the lower fight–flight–freeze centers of my brain and vibrated in my joints and other connecting tissues of my body which told my brain where I was in time and space, and thus signaled it to slow down.

What are restful, soft, slow, rhythmic sounds that a child's ears can hear during sleep time that won't keep them aroused, but lull them into the sleep state? The ebb and flow of the ocean's tide? Native American drumming? An oscillating fan? A metronome? The resting heartbeat of a mother? Some stuffed animals have heartbeats which children may find comforting. Be sure the heartbeat of these stuffed animals is slow enough to soothe and habilitate. I believe that approximately 60 beats a minute is optimal for helping to slow down and retrain children's brains as they sleep.

I have learned in the practice and teaching of Kundalini Yoga (a trauma-sensitive yoga), that a rhythm of 55–60 beats a minute is meditative; it's a good beat for the ears of the brain to hear and the joints of the body to receive in order for positive words, implanted constructive thought, and contemplative prayer to change and guide the mind in a wonderful way. I recommend praying with children at bedtime. Continue to speak slow, melodic, positive prayers over them as they fall asleep. This is the time the brain is most susceptible to suggestion. I once heard a "preacher" say to her congregation: "You can all go ahead and fall asleep if you want to… For I've got your subconscious!" After that comment, *no one* dozed for the rest of the sermon.

A consistent 60–80 beats a minute helps the brain move off the arousal spectrum. It's a really good beat to have in the background of one's day of activities. Music by Mozart, other slow, non-raucous classical music, and "New Age" music can all meet that criterion.

Ideas for non-sleep time proprioception-enhancing rhythmic play and activities

For children with good balance, jumping with a pogo stick is a fabulous, compensatory activity that jars and stimulates the joints so they can feel the self again and calm down. Children going into hyper-arousal (fight or flight) or hypo-arousal (freeze) from anxiety-provoking circumstances can jump out that anxiety (which, by the way, may look like obsessiveness or oppositional behavior).

Putting a suspected proprioceptively challenged, hypo-vestibular (too fast moving) child on a pogo stick can create enough joint-jarring to bring the vestibular system down to "0," as Judith Bluestone (2003–6) of the HANDLE Approach used to say, so the brain can reboot. Children who are hypo-vestibular (ADHD-looking), moving too fast, and dysregulating, can bounce on a pogo stick until they have no more bounce in them (as long as their balance and muscle tone can support them on the pogo stick). When they get off the pogo stick, they may be a lot more slow moving and pleasant and fun to be around.

The sense of proprioception is supported by the vestibular system. Movement changes the brain, especially movement that jars the joints. If the vestibular system isn't managing anxiety as it should be, turn it off (bring it down to "0"), so that the brain can reboot, much like a computer does.

My father discovered the pogo stick for me when I was in elementary school. I loved it. I jumped and jumped. I utilized all my "excess energy" by pogo-sticking up and down the street where I lived. After bouncing my brains out on that pogo stick, I was slower moving, better thinking, and less annoying to my father. He loved when I used that toy in particular!

Tented areas or small, semi-enclosed areas for proprioceptive security

Just as a tent helps some children sleep better, it also provides a safe, secure place for children to relax enough to get into the smart part of the brain for some focusing and learning.

Years ago, when I was an ESL literacy teacher in the public schools of Houston, Texas, I had a semi-enclosed area made of 3–4-foot-high bookcases where children could retreat to read or complete an individual activity of their choice once they finished their work. The area also worked if kids needed to be left alone for a "chill-out" break. This was long before we understood the significance of neuro-sensory overload. My students at that time were refugees from the civil war in El Salvador. They were all traumatized and somewhere on the fight–flight–freeze continuums most of the time. I realized that sometimes a retreat to an area that was safely cordoned off from the rest of the children and only visible to me, the protector, was, in many cases, what some children needed to rest and refuel so they could rejoin the group.

A pressed po-boy or human sandwich

One type of sandwich made with French bread is called a poor-boy or, as we called it as children, a "po-boy." To make a pressed po-boy, one would press the sandwich between hot irons to toast and flatten it.

My sister and I loved pretending to be the filling that went in between the two pieces of bread. We would get the over-large cushions from the family sofa and put one of the cushions on the floor. One of us would lie, face down, on that cushion then have another cushion put on top of us so that the cushions became the two pieces of bread. Then the person who was not in the sandwich would lie on top of the top cushion (or piece of bread) in order to "press" the "po-boy." I remember how good it felt to be pressed. My sister and I used to argue about who got to be in the sandwich first.

Body vibration activities

Where can children lie face down and feel vibrations coursing through their bodies, vibrating their joints, from something that is making noise, like an oscillating fan or a window-unit air conditioner? As a child, I would lie face down, ear to the footboard of my parents' bed. There was a window-unit air conditioner nearby that vibrated through the wooden floor and into my body. It seemed I could stay there forever. I could add to the reverberation of the headboard by making sounds come out of my mouth that originated from my gut. It was kind of an "aaaaaaah." This activity became a recurrent meditative experience that I frequently revisited on hot, summer days when the air conditioner was hard at work cooling the house.

Hitting a piñata filled with goodies while blindfolded, or pinning the tail on the donkey, are activities that may override the anxiety of not being able to see where one is going. For the traumatized and/or proprioceptively insecure, a towel placed over the head may be less threatening than a blindfold. Some children might also need to feel the safe, secure hands of the providing adult touching their shoulder or back in order to feel at ease enough to participate in any eyes-closed activities.

All eyes-closed activities, even brushing teeth or walking in the dark from one room to the next, can help to train the brain to strengthen the sense of proprioception rather than rely on the visual center to locate items or indicate where the body is in space.

Rhythmic walking, clapping, chanting, and singing
CROSS-LATERAL RHYTHM STICK-TAPPING OR HAND-CLAPPING GAMES

These singing/chanting games are played with a partner. The partners sit or stand across from one another. The purpose is to jar the joints of the hands and arms and compress the joints at the shoulders by having the rhythm sticks or the hands of one partner make contact with the rhythm sticks or the hands of the other partner.

Figure 5.2 Clapping

The hands or hand-held sticks cross one's midline to meet with the partner's hands or rhythm sticks in time to the chanted or sung words (Figure 5.2). As one right hand meets the other's right hand, the partners create a rhythmic synchronicity they can refine through repeated interaction. Rhythmic synchronicity (timely interaction) with others is necessary in social relationships. Cross-lateral means when one appendage (in this case, the arm) crosses the body's midline to the opposite side. When this movement is repetitive, then interhemispheric integration is targeted and should become more efficient. As with most no-tech children's games and activities, more than one neuro-behavioral or socio-emotional strength is supported and emphasized.

People who have fun with each other tend to bond with each other. Hand-clapping and rhythm-stick games can be great games for caregivers to play with traumatized children. They offer non-threatening ways to join with another in cooperative play to simultaneously enjoy something fun. When one's eyes can focus on the other's eyes instead of on the mechanics of the hand clapping or rhythm stick-tapping, the partners subtly deepen their relationship and mutual trust.

Here are the words to a rhythmic, cross-lateral hand-clapping game I played so much as a child that, more than 50 years later, my body (kinesthetic muscle memory) still remembers the rhythmic pattern of the hands, the words, and the tune to the song. I also still remember the joy.

"Under the Bamboo"

Under the Bamboo Tree

True love for you, my darling

True love for me

After we're married,

How happy we will be

Under the Bamboo Tree,

1, 2, 3, Bamboo Tree,

Cha-Cha-Cha, hooray!

With any song or chant accompanied by rhythmic hand-clapping or the proprioceptive joint-jarring tapping of rhythm sticks, maintain a slow, steady beat. Speeding up or slowing down isn't so habilitating for the brain. An optimal consistent rhythm would be 60 to 80 beats a minute. I've even had children and parents practice these games to a metronome to keep the tapping and clapping consistent. If both partners sway and move their bodies in time to the beat, they further practice rhythmic synchronicity, and rhythmic multi-tasking! It's even better for the body and the brain, and it's just more fun!

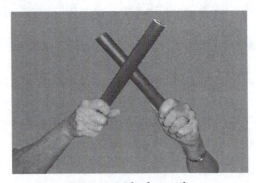

Figure 5.3 Rhythm sticks

Rhythm sticks are easy to make (Figure 5.3). I cut PVC pipe into 12-inch lengths and wrap the pipes in electrical tape of various solid colors. I make green ones, brown ones, red ones, yellow ones, blue ones, and whatever other colors I can find. Striped rhythm sticks are a big no-no for those with weaker vestibular systems. This includes people of my age (as people age, so does the vestibular system) as well as little ones who come from a hurting place. The vestibular system supports the eyes.

LONDON BRIDGE

"London Bridge" is for groups. Two children form the bridge by standing across from each other and interlocking their fingers, one with the other to help with the balance. While everyone sings the song below, the "bridge" children gradually and simultaneously raise and lower their arms all the way up and then all the way down.

In a single file, the other players, or the walkers, walk between the bridge people. They walk slowly, cooperatively, and in rhythm to the song, which has 60 to 80 beats per minute, taking care not to run into the person ahead of them, as they are in single file.

The best time to walk between the "bridge" children is when their arms are all the way up. When the bridge arms are in that position, walkers may not even have to duck to avoid hitting the arms of the bridge. But when the bridge is almost down, the "bridge" children communicate with each other via the words of the song to "lock up" a child who unluckily passed through at the wrong time. The "bridge" children lock arms around that child and gently sway the child back and forth in rhythm to the song.

Here is how we sang it and how the bridge people positioned their hands:

(Arms completely up, forming an upside-down V or chevron, with fingers intertwined):

London Bridge is falling down, falling down, falling down,

London Bridge is falling down, my fair lady.

(Arms with fingers locked in medial position from the ground and slowly moving downward):

London Bridge is half-way down, half-way down, half-way down

London Bridge is half-way down, my fair lady.

(Arms capture, enfold, and sway in time to the words of the song—a walker)

Take the key and lock (him or her) up, lock (him or her) up, lock (him or her) up

Take the key and lock (him or her) up, my fair lady.

(Bridge people release child and drop arms to their sides)

London Bridge has fallen down, fallen down, fallen down,

London Bridge has fallen down, my fair lady.

(Bridge people join hands, link fingers and bring bridge again to a medial position)

London Bridge is half-way up, half-way up, half-way up

London Bridge is half-way up, my fair lady.

(Bridge people with joined hands and intertwined fingers form an upside-down V)

London Bridge is falling down, falling down, falling down,

London Bridge is falling down, my fair lady...

Over and over again, until the players tire of the game.

"London Bridge" is a proprioceptively and rhythmically rich children's cooperation game. For the walkers, it emphasizes "put others first" because they have to be proprioceptively aware of the person in front of or behind them so they don't run over anyone. They also need to be in rhythm with each other.

The children acting as the bridge have to practice proprioceptive awareness of where their arms and bodies are in space. Keeping to the rhythm and beat of the music is important. For traumatized children, being caught and gently swayed in the arms of people with kind smiling faces is not such a bad thing...and they always let the walker go. The walker gets to experience no harm upon capture and a certain release. Human closeness is not so threatening.

Card games

SLAP-THE-JACK: AN INTERACTIVE CARD GAME

This fast-paced game enhances attention and focus. It requires two or more players and a deck of playing cards. The dealer equally distributes all cards, face down, to each player. No player looks at any card. One at a time, each player grabs the top card from his pile and places it face up in the middle of the group. Whenever one throws down a Jack, all players scramble to slap it. The first one who slaps the Jack, wins the entire pile of cards in the middle of the floor or table.

Of course, slapping one's hand on top of the cards initiates proprioceptive jarring of the joints in the hand and arm. Players remain in an aroused, yet controlled state with the thinking part of the brain still turned on in order to sustain alertness but manage stress. And it's fun! It's competitive, yet not threatening. This game also encourages shy, timid children to get in there and compete, thereby helping strengthen confidence and courage through competition.

CHAPTER QUESTIONS

1. The brain remembers what the body practices. And practice makes perfect. In the game "Boogers in the Hall" what, in your opinion, would be the various Fruits of the Spirit that are being practiced and potentially better internalized?

2. Compare the games and activities from this chapter to the levels of growth in Figure 3.2 from Chapter 3, a modified Maslow's Hierarchy. Which games and activities support which levels? Example: "Boogers in the Hall" supports growth in levels 1, 2, 3, 4, 5. How?

3. Using your knowledge from what you have learned in this chapter, think about how the children's pool game, Marco Polo, involves and practices the sense of proprioception?

4. What are games and activities from your childhood or from what you do with the children in your care now that emphasize proprioception? What about rhythm? Can you think of any more activities you could add to your repertoire after reading this chapter?

5. Do you suspect or know that children in your care have propriocep-
    tive deficits? What are the clues and what do you do to help them feel
    more secure in time and in space?

Chapter 6

Build Emotional Regulation and Self-Control so that the Power of the Will Can Strengthen

Emotional self-regulation is the ability of the brain to control feelings and emotions so that the arousal level is appropriate to the situation.

Example: If a hungry saber-toothed tiger appears out of nowhere and tries to eat a little girl as she is playing a chess game with her dad… She should run!

Since there are no saber-toothed tigers in chess games, then jumping and running in a wild-eyed panic when the chess queen is threatened is likely not a good emotionally regulated response to the situation.

Teaching the smart part of the brain to regulate or override fear

"Now, what are you going to do to keep me from capturing your queen?" my father would ask. I would lower my head, take a deep inhale and murmur, "I don't know." It scared me. It seemed so important that I get it right. Somehow I had to save the queen on the chessboard. Her kingdom depended on it. It was too much responsibility. I associated the queen with the highest maternal figure in a castle, a place where a family lived. The home I lived in could be a castle, I supposed. And I guess I was the highest maternal figure in it since I felt as though it was up to me to keep everyone in it safe. Too much stress. Although I felt like running,

I didn't. Instead, I got fidgety and antsy…couldn't sit still. I was only about seven or eight years old.

With no idea what was going on in my head as I transferred the chess game into my own real world, my father would connect with me using his eyes and say, "You are never in a corner that you can't get out of. All you have to do is think. What's the first thing you should do to protect your queen (or myself as I felt)?" I wanted to grab the queen and run. But I didn't.

My father broke down the thinking steps for me. "What's the first thing you should do to defend your queen?"

Of course, I'm translating that subconsciously *to defend myself.* "I don't know."

"Yes, you do. Just think."

He even had me repeat what he said: "Yes, I do. Just think."

He had caught me at an arousal level where I could still turn back toward the thinking, smart part of the brain. His appropriate intervention in order to derail a growing panic came at the right time.

I naturally took deep breaths because he took deep breaths as he stayed with me throughout the thinking process. He ceased being my opponent on the chessboard and became my coach. When I made a bad decision with a pawn or a knight, he never beheaded me or locked me in a tower. My father just said that it wouldn't work and showed me why it wouldn't. I got a second or a third or maybe even a fourth chance to get it right! I would finally succeed. I saved the queen.

Playing chess, my father helped me use the smart part of my brain to cognitively (think) override the aroused and scared non-thinking reactive part of my brain. I have no idea if he knew that was what he was doing at the time…but he was making me stronger. He was building my character and my brain. He was strengthening my ability to regulate my emotions (not go into complete terror) and control my impulses (not jump up and run). He wasn't going to let me give up. He made me have courage. He also wasn't angry or frustrated with me for making mistakes or feeling frightened. He was making the smart part of my brain, or the impulse control center, practice restraint and resilience. His words, his determination, his belief in my innate intelligence and his calmness kept me in my seat and problem-solving until my brain could get to a calmer place, and I could do my best thinking.

How better control of the emotions leads to better self-control and better self-control leads to better self-discipline: And all that leads us back to the Fruit of the Spirit...

Self-control

Self-control occurs when the thinking part of the brain is able to jump in and be the boss of the impulses and emotions rising up from the lower reaches of the brain. It's about restraining the body and/or the mouth from doing something it shouldn't. Anyone remember the expression, "Open mouth, insert foot"? The better the smart part of the brain can control (regulate) emotions and the better the emotions can be regulated by the smart part of the brain, then the better the self-control becomes. It's a two-way street. When brain circuits are doing a good job connecting the thinking and non-thinking parts of the brain, then emotions can be better regulated and impulses can be better controlled.

Example: When a little eight-year-old girl feels the extreme urge to physically get up and run from a chess game and bring the queen with her, but doesn't, then some self-control is in place. (She instead gets "ants in her pants" and starts moving and fidgeting in attempts to distract herself from the fear that is increasing...but at least she stays in her seat!)

Self-discipline

When someone practices self-control until it becomes a habit, it's called self-discipline. Self-discipline is the end result of practiced self-control which has built upon practiced regulation of the emotions. Consistently practiced self-discipline results in stronger will or willpower. Willpower is conscious determination.

Example: The more the little girl practices overriding strong emotions that prevent her from running from a chess game and "staying present" (in the smart part of the brain), the more self-control she develops to override fear. The more she practices self-control, the more self-disciplined she can become.

"There's no such word as 'can't,'" my father would say. "You just have to want to." In his eyes, repetitive chess playing helped people develop self-discipline, and the ability to problem-solve even under pressure. He believed chess was "initial boot camp training" to help people think on their feet and cognitively override emotions that prevented them from doing so. He was right, even though he didn't know that people had to be caught at a time on the arousal spectrum when they could still be turned around. That said, he was still helping me practice the art of emotional restraint.

Impulses that result in actions start in the lower, non-thinking part of the brain. The smart part of the brain needs regular practice regulating impulses (desires and feelings) that don't do anyone any good. When self-control is strong enough, it can be powered by willpower. The prerequisite to that feat is dependable, strong communication between the smart and non-smart parts (higher and lower parts) of the brain, so that arousal, or emotions can be controlled. When one has a functional, brakes-on-or-off smart part of the brain that can and does say "no" to unnecessary arousal and unhealthy emotions, urges, and impulses, then one's character can consistently demonstrate the Fruit of the Spirit.

When emotional regulation, self-control, and strength of will aren't strong enough: The woeful tale of David and the family pickup truck

One day, a couple received bad news of a family tragedy. Throughout the day mom was crying; dad was slamming things and "grumping." Son David, a sensitive 13-year-old, felt his parents' stress. Although he didn't know that his parents had received bad news, he felt ill at ease because his beloved parents were out of sorts.

David was also fetal alcohol- and drug-affected and had been adopted as a toddler. The in utero drugs and alcohol his birth mother consumed caused him serious after-birth emotional self-regulation problems. His first adoptive placement failed because he cried and screamed most of the time. So David ended up with a family who had the finances and the strength of will to do what they had to do to help him become all he could be.

At age 13, David was still learning disabled, and he still had lots of problems regulating his emotions when under significant stress. The brakes in the smart part of his brain worked…sometimes, as long as he wasn't under too much stress. When the thinking part of his brain was working, he was amazingly altruistic. He was a child of good character. He demonstrated the Fruit of the Spirit.

David was a big boy, and when he was in his right mind, he was a gentle giant. But if he wasn't in his "right mind" he could lose control, fast, and become completely irrational and a harm to himself and to others. When he returned to a calm state, he would be totally remorseful for what he had done. He had the desire to please when the thinking part of his brain was in charge, but not when he had lost his mind. Then he was a maniac.

On the day his parents were reacting to the family tragedy, David did what he frequently did to soothe himself. His go-to compensatory behavior was to allow one of the family dogs to lick his face. The facial massage from the dog's tongue calmed him and helped to relax an important cranial nerve on his face, the trigeminal nerve. When the trigeminal nerve is relaxed, then the lower part of the brain is better able to relax.

David's dad, who wasn't managing his own lower reactive brain state very well, saw David on the floor, eyes closed, completely absorbed in the great tongue massage he was getting from the family pet. David's dad quietly sneaked up behind David, thumped his head harshly with his middle finger and yelled "Stop it; that's gross."

David jolted out of his altered state, rose up in a swelling rage to yell at and curse his father. The more dad wouldn't disengage, the more David's rage increased. Initially, David had enough wherewithal to try and leave the room; however, dad kept following him, blocking his departure, while futilely trying to defend his position that dogs shouldn't lick human faces.

Dad messed up…big time, from the beginning.

By this time, David was out of his mind. He went to the garage and threw a chair through the windshield of his father's car. Seeing the keys in the family pickup truck, David raced off, even though he had never before driven a vehicle. In his state of mind, and with his lack of driving ability, he was dangerous.

Eventually someone found David parked at a gas station. He didn't know where he was. Though no physical harm had come to anyone, David was scared, remorseful, and couldn't remember what had happened. He asked over and over again what was wrong with him…why did he do the things he did?

Dos and don'ts for caregivers: Thou shalt not make a bad situation worse for those who have emotional regulation problems

How should David's dad have handled the situation differently? First, *he* should have exercised more emotional regulation, self-control, and self-awareness! Because dad was upset by bad news, he took it out on David. He should have gotten himself into a better place before interacting with any family members, including the dog.

Never sneak up on anyone who has problems with hyper-arousal, or known problems with emotional brain regulation. Announce your approach, especially when the brain-traumatized person is in a relaxed, altered state. In that state they are most vulnerable and reactive. Their guard is down. Just ask war veterans.

Never touch a traumatized person from behind, without announcing your presence. Always avoid any harsh, unseen, or unkind physical touch to any part of the traumatized person's body.

When seeing David's initial reaction to his comment, Dad should have realized he had done something totally out of line and worked to correct the situation immediately. Instead, he made it worse by following David and defending his own position. In that state, David couldn't take in any information. He tried to leave the room as a coping method to avoid complete dysregulation (insanity). Dad's persistent arguing and blocking his son's attempt to "flee" accelerated his son's downward dive into emotional disintegration. David went "nuts." No one was "driving" David's body or mouth, and his braking system, which was already impaired, was non-operational.

The old saying, "If you can't say anything nice, don't say anything at all," would have been much more appropriate here. After initially disrupting his son, dad should have at least stopped, breathed, halted all movement (including his mouth), postured his body in a non-defensive, non-threatening stance, softened his face, and just shut down operation. It would have been David's only chance, however slight, of re-regulating himself when not under such continued, doggedly persistent threat.

Building the braking system of the brain and slowing down the reaction

Better communication between the lower, reactive regions of the brain and the smart part of the brain results in better regulation of emotions and impulses. As stated in Chapter 2, the more organized the brain circuitry is between the higher and lower regions of the brain (thinking and non-thinking), the more control people have over what they say and do, especially under perceived threat.

If one can switch on and then off a behavior instead of getting stuck in a downward free fall into the depths of madness and despair, then one probably has fairly good brakes controlling the smart part of the brain. Consistently suppressing reflexive actions such as not automatically hitting back when someone hits first, or smashing a car windshield with a chair when upset, indicates some type of functional braking system.

The more organized the brain is, the more a person has control of it. When one's brain has matured to the point that it can direct a part of the body to stay still and cease involuntary movement of other unnecessary body parts (overflow of movement), better brain control is developing. Reading by moving one's entire head rather than just the eyes is an example of overflow of movement. I even had an uncle who, when driving, would stick out his tongue to the left when he turned the car to the left, and then stick out his tongue to the right when he turned right. I don't think his tongue was helping the car turn.

Judith Bluestone (2003–6), referred to the brain process that suppressed unnecessary movement, or overflow of body parts, as *differentiation of response* or *differentiation of movement*. When the brain matures to the point it naturally suppresses unnecessary body movements, then the brain is organizing itself into specialized centers, and the smart part brain brakes work better.

The better organized brain can control arousal levels and be less reactive or reflexive. Thus, a person *can* have better control of emotions and impulses. If the brain is aroused too much of the time (a lower brain response to perceived threat), then the higher or smart part of the brain, where the braking system is supposed to be, can't do its job as well as it needs to.

So, when children display problems with emotional regulation, hyper-activity, self-control, and/or problems getting stuck in (inability to pull out of) a downward descent into emotionally dysregulated hell, therapeutic intervention should start at least at the level of differentiation. This means kids should practice games and activities that not only exercise the on/off switch or brake and release system, but also the isolation of body parts to perform certain tasks.

Rhythm may help refine the brain's braking system

Researchers at Gilden Lab at the University of Texas have conducted successful studies (Gilden and Marusich 2009) showing that participants diagnosed with ADHD experience the world on a faster time scale than those who do not have a diagnosis of ADHD. Perhaps if children with emotional regulation, attention issues, and self-control problems practice activities that slow down their inner timing, then their mental timing might slow down as well. With their mental timing slowed, maybe their acceleration into the no man's land part of the brain can be slowed down as well. If their brains were fed a steady diet of slower, consistent rhythm, and they performed activities at a slower, consistent rhythm, then perhaps that slower consistent rhythm could help the process of differentiation better mature, so that interhemispheric integration and brain control could improve.

I wonder about the rhythmic heartbeat of David's birth mom that bathed him before he was born? Was it rhythmic at all? Or was it all over the place due to her stress level and whatever it was she ingested to control her anxiety?

If an unborn child's brain had been bathed by the heartbeat of a calm, predominantly regulated gestational heart, then could not the child's brain have had nine months of effective, healthy brain training before the child's eyes ever saw the light of day? Children with inferior in utero brain training by the mother's gestational heartbeat need rehabilitation. Their brains need to receive, and their bodies need to replicate, the desired beat of a calm, gestational heart. The rhythm may gradually adjust and slow children's impulse control problems, better organize their brain, and improve emotional regulation and self-control. After all, practice makes perfect.

Games and activities to help build better braking, better differentiated, more rhythmic brains

60-beat-a-minute rhythm and rhyme choosing games to decide who goes first or becomes "it" in a game or activity

ONE POTATO, TWO POTATO

To begin, all players stand or sit in a circle and make fists to form potatoes. When the leader says, "Put your potatoes in," players extend both fists into the circle. The leader, designated the "chooser," taps everyone's potatoes, including his own, while rhythmically chanting:

"One potato, two potato, three potato, four

Five potato, six potato, seven potato, more."

The fist tapped at "more" must withdraw from the circle and go behind the back of the person to whom it is attached. The person with the last potato left in the circle becomes either "it" or gets to go first in whatever game or activity that is to be played. It was common for the potato tapper to move and sway to the rhythm of the chant.

ENGINE, ENGINE, NUMBER 9

This choosing game is a variation of *One Potato, Two Potato*. It's played the same way, but to a longer, more varied song.

"Engine, Engine, Number 9

Going down Chicago line

If the train should jump the track

Would you get your money back

Spoon, knife, fork, you!"

Both choosing games help the participants practice isolation of body parts, focus, and waiting. The tapping of the fists also gives children some proprioceptive input.

Paired, in sync movement that is slow and consistent to a 60-beat-a-minute-rhythm

Below are some activities I've taught my caregivers to do with their children:

- Drum tapping to a clock or to a metronome

- Partnered rhythm stick or hand-clapping games to songs and chants

- Marching in time to a metronome, to someone hand-clapping, or to the beating of a drum

- Marching in time with a partner to the beat of a metronome or a drum, either behind or next to the partner

Activities that require waiting and impulse control (practice in slowing it down)

TIMED PLAY

Timed play helps children practice longer, focused play. A timer is used to slow down children and keep them from racing from one toy box to another without thoroughly examining the contents of any box nor really playing with anything that's inside. It's about delaying gratification and slowing the brain down.

Limit the timing for whatever is reasonable for the developmental age of the child. When the timer goes off, the child may choose to stay with the same box or explore another. Add lots of praise for the child who successfully plays until the timer goes off. Add a minute or two to each timed session until the child's attention span and impulse control ability reaches something closer to the desired developmental level.

TBRI® (Trust-Based Relational Intervention) creators Dr. David Cross and the late Dr. Karyn Purvis indicated in their book *The Connected Child* (2007) and emphasize in the TBRI® trainings

(Purvis *et al.* 2013), that new behaviors come on line faster with an element of fun. Sometimes an attitude of "I bet you can't do it" entices children to show that they can. Consistent praise for staying with the game plan may be effective, too. I've also noticed that some children will work for food! If a successful tasty incentive to stay with a game plan of slowing down the rapid search for more toys, for example, results in a tasty blueberry or other form of fruit or low carb candy, then so be it.

RE-DOS TO HELP THE BODY PRACTICE IMPULSE CONTROL

Doctors Karyn Purvis and David Cross's trainings and literature (2007) endorse re-dos as effective activities for brain training. If children practice the right way to do something enough, then the right way become habit, a part of the body's kinesthetic or muscle memory. Judith Bluestone, of The HANDLE Approach, said individuals with immature differentiation may have a weakness in kinesthetic memory. These children may need more repetitive practice for targeted skills to become automatic.

Purvis' and Cross' approach to successful re-dos differs from how I remember as a child. At school, if we children ran wildly down the hall, a teacher blew a loud whistle and made us start the entire procession again, this time slow, dignified, and orderly. It wasn't fun.

The work of Purvis and Cross, and Bluestone, emphasizes that brain learning made fun and enjoyable perfects skills faster. So, when kids re-do and get it right, celebrate enthusiastically.

Stop-go games and activities (braking, acceleration, and waiting with some isolation of body parts)

RED LIGHT, GREEN LIGHT

In this game, one player tries to notice other children moving instead of being still. When caught, the "movers" are eliminated from play before touching the one in charge.

One player acts as the traffic light by standing close to, and facing, one wall (or fence or imaginary border). All the other children stand against the opposite wall (the greater the distance between the traffic light and the other players, the longer the game can last).

While still facing the wall, the traffic light says "green light" to cue the other children to begin running toward the light. Then, as the traffic light is turning to face the runners, he says "red light" to cue the players to stop and freeze. Any player that the traffic light sees running or moving body parts is eliminated from the game.

The traffic light repeats the same process, with each runner unfreezing and moving forward again. The runner who touches the traffic light first gets to be the traffic light next.

This game reinforces self-control, body part control, and braking.

When the brain can practice starting and stopping on someone else's command, the person with that brain is more likely to be able to do so in a real emergency when someone yells "Stop!" or "Run!" Further, runners get practice in obediently stopping all body part movement for an undetermined period of time based upon how much the traffic light wants to keep players in freeze mode. The brain and body practice obeying authority.

SWING THE STATUE
Instructions for this game's rules and benefits appear in Chapter 2.

MOTHER, MAY I?
This is an outdoor game played on a court, a driveway, or even a field. The caller, "Mother," stands facing a group of children who stand behind an imaginary line facing her. If a male is the caller, the game can be "Father, May I?"

One by one, "Mother" instructs each child to complete a physical movement. Before moving, the child must ask "Mother, may I?" and wait for "Mother" to reply "Yes, you may" before moving as instructed. The "Mother" gives a different command to another player. With each successfully performed request, "Mother" should make the subsequent request a little harder. The objective is for each child to move successfully through the challenges until physically reaching where "Mother" is standing.

This game has many benefits. It gently challenges children to increase their ability to focus, listen, and remember the sequence of aural instructions. It also helps children exercise their braking system and practice physical, organized sequencing of movement which is brain organizing.

Further, if the children's actual parent is "Mother" or "Father," then the children get practice obeying that parent when they're asked to do something, the first time they're asked. It helps caregivers establish benevolent authority.

FREEZE TAG

Another outside game, Freeze Tag, has whoever is "It" to chase and tag runners. When tagged, the runner must freeze. To unfreeze, a runner must be tagged by another runner who isn't frozen. The game ends when all the runners have been tagged.

Though simple to play, this game is mentally constructive. Not only must children sharpen the stop/go mechanism in their brains, but must also figure out where and how to run to escape the tagger. The game requires multi-tasking and planned, non-impulsive, non-frantic cause–effect thinking (what a perfect set up for the next chapter on interhemispheric integration). Also, children must practice "being a friend" and tagging fellow runners to unfreeze them. That's practice being a hero and putting others first, a Fruit of the Spirit characteristic.

THE HOT LAVA GAME

This game can be fun indoors if the room has no breakable items and has been fairly child-proofed. Players pretend that the floor is covered with hot lava. They must carefully maneuver their way around that lava and not get any of their body parts burned due to contact. Throw pillows can represent stepping stones, and furniture can be something they climb on as they make their way through or around the lava. If burned, they are off the playing field and must try again when it is their next turn.

This game encourages players to practice planned cause–effect thinking (necessary for good interhemispheric integration) and rewards this effective pre-movement problem-solving. Careful movement of only the body parts needed to maintain balance is an optimal goal. Children have to be aware of where their bodies are in time and in space (proprioception). They must practice moving slowly and cautiously. And they have to practice determination and belief in their innate ability to make it through life's challenges!

BLIND MAN'S BLUFF

This game requires at least three players and is played outside or inside where there are places to hide and within reasonable distance of a blindfolded "It." "It" spins around five times. While "It" spins, the other players quickly search for hiding places. When "It" stops spinning and yells "freeze," the players stop moving. "It" then searches for the hidden, non-noise-making players. The players may avoid "It" by moving their upper body parts out of the way as "It" approaches, but they may not move their feet, which are planted, nor make a sound because their lower bodies are frozen. The last person to be found is the next "It."

Whether playing inside or outside, players should take care that the blindfolded "It" not get hurt due to lack of vision. Whoever is "It" should have a fairly well-functioning vestibular system (balance) and sense of proprioception to prevent them from wandering off into the great unknown and never being seen nor heard from again. "It's" sense of proprioception is further improved by this game.

The other players are highly motivated only to move the body parts that may need movement to avoid detection and to isolate and restrain the lower part of the body from movement. What a fun way to practice the braking system of isolated body parts!

RED ROVER, RED ROVER

This game requires many players. Two lines of children face each other across a small, open running field. The children of each line hold the hands of the children on either side of them. One side chants one time, "Red Rover, Red Rover, send (child's name) right over."

The child called from the other side then runs as hard as she can toward the opposing side's chain. Acting as a battering ram, she attempts to break through one link of the chain, forcing two joined hands to disconnect. If the child succeeds, she selects any player for that chain to join her chain. If she fails to break the link, the child joins the opposing side and becomes part of their chain. In the end, the side with the most players wins.

Who excels at this game? Actually, the child with the weakest on or off switch makes the best battering ram because she doesn't slow down at all upon approach. The children in the chain that child rams full-force must control their arousal state to keep their hands linked. They must be aware of what their posture and facial affect is saying to the runner. They want to appear strong and impermeable. Because it includes many players, this game takes time and requires patience as children wait their turn to be called.

HOT POTATO

The more kids in this game, the merrier. Players stand in a circle and toss a round object (or an actual potato), one person to the next, while music is playing. The player holding the potato when the music stops is eliminated. The player not holding the potato when the music stops stays in the game. Via elimination, the winner will be the last one standing with no potato.

The potato tosser has to wait for the next person in the circle to be ready to receive. If the tosser carelessly throws the potato without waiting for that person to be ready and the potato falls, then the tosser may be eliminated due to carelessness. Also, if a tosser tries to rid himself of the potato by throwing it at the next person when the music stops, then he may be eliminated, too. Impulsivity isn't rewarded in this game; "other" awareness is. The winner gets to start and stop the music for the next round.

MUSICAL CHAIRS

This game follows the same concept as "Hot Potato" but on a grander scale because the props are larger and more numerous. Cluster chairs, facing outward, in the middle of the room. There should always be one fewer chair than there are players. (If ten children are playing, start with nine chairs.) Someone begins some music, which prompts all the players to walk around the cluster of chairs. As soon as the music stops, players scramble to sit in a chair. The one player who did not sit down is eliminated. Remove one chair each round and continue the game until the last child in the final round sits in the only remaining chair and wins. The winner controls the music in the next round.

If two children sit down on one chair at absolutely the same time, will it be a fight to the finish or will one child give up their seat to the other out of kindness? Certainly, there should be some type of reward or at least praise for the child who puts the other one first. This game encourages attention, focus, braking, rhythmic, in sync walking with others, control of the emotions, and perhaps altruism.

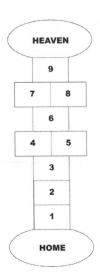

Figure 6.1 Hopscotch

To set up the game, draw a numbered grid (see Figure 6.1) with chalk on concrete or with a stick on dirt. To begin play, the first player tosses a stone onto square 1. The player must hop past any square containing the stone and then land with one foot on a single square or with both feet simultaneously on side-by-side squares. The top of the hopscotch has a circle called Heaven, where the player may land with both feet. It is a resting place. Once there, the player turns around and hops, single- or double-square at a time, back toward the start. When reaching square 2, the player bends on one foot to pick up the stone on square 1. The child then jumps on the cleared square 1, and on one foot turns around, and tosses the stone onto square 2 to begin the journey to Heaven and back again. The goal is to get all the way to Heaven and back to square 1 without stepping on a line, losing balance, or tossing the stone into an unintended area. If a child errs, he surrenders his turn to the next player, but may try to master the hopscotch grid again after everyone has had a turn. The winner is the first player to hop to Heaven and back with the stone having been on each square.

Hopscotch is a thinking and planning anti-impulsive movement game that requires advanced differentiation of movement, start/stop rhythmic jumping, and balance. A child's vestibular system (inner ear) should be strong enough so the child can balance on one foot while simultaneously bending over and picking up a stone.

The game also demands patience, as children must wait their turn because only one child at a time can be on the hopscotch grid.

Even for children with math anxiety, seeing numbers in squares shouldn't be intimidating. The game requires no counting or adding or subtracting. Numbers only indicate sequential order, which helps to orient children linearly in time and space. Too many children try to go too fast at this game. In order to win, the child has to get all the way to Heaven and back to the initial starting point without messing up.

RACING GAMES: "ON YOUR MARKS, GET SET, GO!"

Whether children are foot racing, human wheelbarrow racing, or potato sack racing, start–stop racing games are excellent brain-training exercises for children. Not only can children's brains become better organized because they are practicing immediate start/stop movements on someone else's command, but they are good practice for habit making: children need to practice starting and stopping on someone's command for the purpose of their own safety in case of emergency.

Short of firing a pistol to get excited kids' attention when the race begins or ends, caregivers should think of using what they would use in the home or at school or daycare to signal an immediate "stop" or "go." What noise-interrupting method does the caregiver habitually use to immediately get a child's attention when the quiet glance or the index finger raised up in the air has failed? The commanding voice, the clapping of hands, a whistle? The caregiver should use whatever method she already uses to get children to stop everything they're doing and give her their undivided attention. What the body practices, the brain remembers.

CHILDREN'S HATHA YOGA

Live hatha yoga group classes that include focused breath and meditation can offer children (and adults) an opportunity to practice self-awareness, emotional self-regulation, self-control, and self-discipline.

The yogic practice of slowing down and lengthening the breath can help children practice modulating the arousal state. Holding yogic positions can help children increase slowing down and impulse control. Holding of yogic positions, combined with controlling the breath helps people become more aware of their bodies and themselves, and helps their brains practice more control of their minds. Some hatha yoga poses are similar to neuro-behavioral movement strategies to help early reflexes integrate as they should.

Our level of anxiety shows up in the speed and rhythm of our speech and in our physical body movement. We tend to move and speak in time to our breath.

The chronically anxious breathe in short, upper body, dysrhythmic breaths, instead of long, deep rhythmic belly breaths. People who typically breathe in short, dysrhythmic, choppy breaths tend to move choppily and dysrhythmically as well. They often speak rapidly with an unnecessary overflow of body parts (shuffling their feet, moving their shoulders up and down as they sit and talk) that constantly move when they should be still. Practicing longer, deeper breaths can relax anxious people. Over time, it may help them become less chronically or acutely emotionally and behaviorally reactive, and less unnecessarily aroused.

Research confirms that yoga practice has a positive role in healing trauma. Noted psychiatrist and trauma researcher, Dr. Bessel van der Kolk and colleagues showed that ten weeks of yoga practice markedly reduced the PTSD symptoms of patients who had failed to respond to any other treatment, including medication (van der Kolk *et al.* 2014).

TWISTER®

This physical body game, introduced in 1966, requires players to place their hand or foot on a colored circle indicated by the spin of a dial. After multiple spins, players end up in contorted positions, either over or under other players, which they are required to hold for an undetermined period of time (which can seem like forever!). The player able to reach every colored circle indicated and hold the position the longest, wins.

This game is excellent for helping children control body parts, move cautiously and utilize planned, cause–effect thinking to place their bodies in positions they can hold, so they don't cause themselves nor others to fall (other awareness). For the traumatized, it also helps them lose their fear of being physically close to others because they are having such a good time being silly.

Fine motor games and activities (games that require practice and coordination of isolation of body parts, patience and rhythmic timing)

OPERATION®

Cavity Sam lies on the operating table with several ailments that can be cured by surgically removing small objects from cavities on his body. Players pick a card indicating which object to remove, then must remove it with metal tweezers without touching the metal sides of the cavity which causes a small vibration, triggers a comical buzzing, and turns Sam's lightbulb nose red.

To make the game more developmentally challenging, have children practice breathing deeply in and out while using only the body parts necessary to control the tweezers. Tongues sticking out of mouths don't help the fingers guide the tweezers to their destination. Facial grimacing, shuffling feet, or fidgeting bodies don't help guide tweezers, either.

FINGER PUPPETS

Figure 6.2 Finger puppet play, such as "Where Is Thumpkin?"

Children's fingers don puppets and practice isolating and moving those fingers to rhythmic song (Figure 6.2).

Note: Finger puppet movement means just that. If whole arms and whole bodies are not a part of the finger play song, then those body parts unnecessary to the play should refrain from moving.

It's okay if children need assistance holding down fingers or balancing the arm that shouldn't move along with the targeted finger. In time, those children will be able to mentally restrain the unneeded fingers or whatever other body part wants to play and shouldn't.

YouTube videos include many finger play songs, including different versions of "Where Is Thumpkin?" For children just learning the task by watching the video, choose a version with a slow, soothing rhythm and beat. Once they've learned finger plays from videos, children should practice the exercises with another person, preferably the caregiver. Encourage smiles, eye contact, and other social connections that lead to greater enjoyment and trust.

PICK UP STICKS

This is another inside game to keep kids busy, out of trouble, and training their brains. Although you could buy the Pick up Sticks game, you may as easily use ice cream sticks, thin tongue depressors, chopsticks, shish kabob skewers, or any thin elongated sticks of the same width and length.

The object of the game is to remove a single target stick from a pile without disturbing the other sticks. To begin the game, someone gently drops a fistful of sticks onto a table or onto the floor. Each player takes a turn slowly and carefully removing a target stick from the pile without disturbing any other stick. (In some versions, players use their fingers. In others, they use one stick to remove the target stick.) Successful players get to keep the stick they remove. Unsuccessful attempts require players to leave that stick in the pile. The winner is the player with the most sticks at the end of the game.

There are many variations of the game. Some people keep score by awarding sticks of certain colors a point value. Children who developmentally aren't ready to move sticks with a stick should be allowed to pick up a stick with their fingers…just the pincer grasp, for example.

To succeed at this game, children must discipline only the body parts needed to perform the task. Children also practice focusing mental attention on the task, slowing down, and applying some cause–effect thinking. Children may need to be reminded to breathe slowly and deeply as they concentrate on moving their sticks. That aids grace of movement and reduces anxiety which may reduce overflow movement of body parts. Also, when children have to get up, change the position of their head and body to better pick up a stick, they are very likely giving their vestibular system a little workout. When the vestibular system (inner ear) is gently boosted by movement, it can better support all higher brain functions that depend on it.

JACKS

Figure 6.3 Jacks

This is a good indoor game that must be played on an uncarpeted floor. To begin, cup all the jacks in one hand and gently drop them all in the same general area (Figure 6.3). Players use one hand to bounce a small rubber ball, scoop up a jack or jacks, and catch the ball before it bounces twice. As each scoop is gathered and before the ball is bounced again for the next scoop, the playing hand transfers the scooped jack or jacks over to the other hand to hold.

Each round, players increase the number of jacks they scoop. At "onesies," the player bounces the ball, scoops up one jack, and catches the ball before the second bounce. After each player has successfully mastered the "onesies," he then moves on to "twosies," then "threesies," and onward until all the jacks can be scooped up at once before the ball bounces twice.

The players who make it to the end, win.

New-to-the-game players won't master "onesies" until they can bounce the ball properly, pick up a jack, and catch the ball again.

Beginners have to practice grading of movement (not bouncing the ball too hard), learning how to toss the ball so they have time to retrieve jacks and catch the ball after only one bounce (timing). It takes focused visual observance to see that they are to toss the ball up and let it bounce rather than throw it down to bounce. Let kinesthetic learners follow the bouncing ball up by moving their chins upward with the ball to help them get the movement in their body. Players also have to follow a linear sequence which is brain organizing: toss the ball up, scoop the jacks, catch the ball, then transfer the jacks to the other hand. It is important to let children practice "onesies" until they master the task, before moving on to higher-numbered rounds.

Nowadays, it's difficult to find heavy metal jacks. Lightweight plastic jacks don't do a thing for someone with a diminished sense of proprioception. The heavier the jacks, the happier the sense of proprioception.

This game practices kinesthetic memory (muscle memory) of the body, so that the body remembers what it is supposed to do, and so that the mind doesn't have to remind it. This game also gives practice in training selective body parts to respond accordingly in a timely, rhythmic manner. Some children with immature differentiation have less than efficient kinesthetic memory. This game provides great practice for developing that skill.

Children need a lot of help and encouragement with this game, so they don't frustrate and quit playing.

MARBLE GAMES

There are many variations of marble games that can be played indoors or out. In whatever version children play, they must learn to hold the marble correctly between the index finger and thumb so they shoot or "flick," not push the marble. When shooting, children must learn to use only their thumb, not their entire arm. It certainly is undifferentiated to move the whole arm to shoot a marble when only the index finger and thumb of one hand are necessary for the task. Only the thumb moves on a hand that shoots a marble.

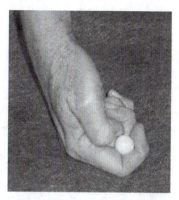

Figure 6.4 Marble shooting

Children can play marbles with a homemade shooting gallery that's as fun to make as it is to play (Figure 6.4). Cut and number several openings in a shoebox or larger box without flaps, and place the box upside down. Players get on their hands and knees behind a line and try to shoot a marble through the numbered openings. Each opening number equals the score players get when their marble goes through it. The winner is the player with the highest score.

This game helps players not only refine body part movement and practice fine motor skills (properly holding and shooting marbles with special attention to the thumb as a power source), but it also enhances hand/eye coordination and requires practicing simple math (adding of numbers) in a fun, tangible way (Figure 6.5).

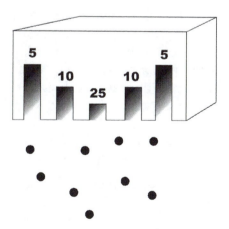

Figure 6.5 Marble game

FINGER STRING GAMES

Figure 6.6 Finger string games

What a fun activity to do indoors on a rainy or cold day, or at school during break time! Finger string games (Figure 6.6) are exactly what they're called: alone or with a partner, children create different designs with string (or elastic) woven through their fingers. Playing as partners, one child can show the other how to make one kind of art, or both could practice what they both know in order to perfect it. Generally, the activity is so meditative and calming that, without realizing it, children's breath will follow the graceful weaving in and out of their fingers through the strings.

The Internet offers many string designs with simple step-by-step instructions to make them. Once learned, the designs often imprint on children's memories. As a child, I made Cup and Saucer so many times that I can still make the design because my fingers (kinesthetic memory) still know what to do without my having to think about it.

This play sharpens mental focus and concentration while providing a way to connect (literally) with others, face to face (or hand to hand when a design is joined with someone else's fingers). In order to master a design, children must get their fingers to obey their minds. This helps children practice putting the smart part of the brain in charge of the body. It also helps with sequential, logical order: step by step, the fingers have to perform manipulation of the string or elastic in the order that would produce the design.

Although children might become frustrated if their fingers can't initially create a design, the desire to master the relatively simple task usually overrides their frustration. This process invites children to not give up, and to become aware of negative, self-defeating feelings so they can push through them.

YO-YO PLAY

What fun a yo-yo is. What self-control and self-discipline it brings. How wonderful a heavy yo-yo (with a decent string) feels proprioceptively. Yo-yoing can be a solitary act that a child enjoys, and it may be brain calming or meditative.

Through repetitive, slow rhythm, the yo-yo helps the brain practice the simple skill of making it cascade down and spin back up its string. One can't make a yo-yo go any faster than it goes. Often children will slow their breath to match the yo-yo's soothing purr and often hypnotic rhythm.

Children should get yo-yos that are heavy; lighter ones are usually cheaply made and cause frustration because they don't move smoothly. Avoid yo-yos with gaudy designs. The vestibular system has a hard time supporting the eyes when there is a sea of swirling color going up and down a string. Play doesn't last too long with a yo-yo that hurts the eyes or makes someone feel dizzy, nauseated, or grouchy. A solid color yo-yo, or close to it, is best.

Before they attempt to learn yo-yo tricks, give children time and encouragement to master the ascension and descension of the yo-yo, and the flick of the wrist required (body part isolation). If they don't modify their breath to match the up and down movement of the yo-yo, you can remind them.

CHAPTER QUESTIONS

1. What are some activities and games you can think of that can help children improve self-regulation and self-control? Why?

2. What do you think horseback riding can do to help children's brains?

3. What are some choosing games you remember from childhood?

4. Have you ever taken a yoga class? What was your experience?

5. What do you think would be the benefits (socio-emotionally and neuro-behaviorally) of tai kwon do for children?

6. Can you think of any more activities that could help children practice the isolation of body parts?

7. What are some finger string designs you remember? Bring some string or elastic and teach the others in your class if that is where you are reviewing this chapter.

Chapter 7

Build Courage, Compassion, and Higher-Level Thinking through Problem-Solving Activities and Acts of Bravery

Courage, common sense, and altruism

Courage

Courage is the strength of God within that helps one say or do what is just and good. It requires overriding, with character and common sense, the fear that would prevent one from acting. It often requires feeling fear and acting anyway because something significant has to be stopped or something important has to start. The process of making it happen or not happen may not be pleasant.

People develop courage over time with the support and mentoring of courageous caregivers and with life's experiences that children witness, and in which children participate. Those life experiences can be real crises when children experience others acting courageously. They can also be the experiences that children create in their imaginative play where they become their own heroes or heroines and determine their own positive outcomes.

Common sense

Common sense is a developed ability that enables people to make good, logical, thought-out decisions so that acts of courage and courses of action are more decisive and effective. People can make better common sense decisions when they have had enough real-world problem-solving opportunities to be able to transfer problem-solving steps practiced from the known experiences to the unknown experiences. Common sense problem-solving ability has been referred to as "connecting the dots" or having the ability to go from "A to B to C to D." People can make better common sense decisions if their brains have had experience in practicing the control of impulses and emotions and doing serious thinking, even under pressure.

Caregivers must give children developmentally appropriate experiences in problem-solving. My father did when teaching me chess. The mother in Chapter 3 did when she helped her adoptive daughter organize cans of English peas for the family's general store.

This task made the daughter feel proud of herself, encouraged her to feel safer and more secure in her new home, and helped her develop organizational skills that she could transfer to other settings, such as organizing her bedroom.

Practicing certain skills improves related skills required to perform other similar tasks. In "real-world," face-to-face creative and neuro-behavioral play with others, children practice problem-solving, cause–effect, common sense thinking repeatedly in a fun context. Skills practiced in an environment of pleasure stand a better chance of becoming permanent fixtures in the brain in less time.

Common sense requires effective interhemispheric integration, or communication between the two sides of the smart part of the brain: the left side and the right side. Effective, interhemispheric integration, with brakes in place, is the neuro-behavioral goal for successful, independent adulthood. A person needs a brain that can and will think, will brake or accelerate on command, and will do a good job in doing so.

Altruism

Altruism results when courage, resiliency, and the Fruit of the Spirit are internalized and put into action. (See Figure 3.2 Level 5, Maturity.)

Altruism is the Fruit of the Spirit character goal for successful adulthood. It represents the highest act of selflessness and obedience to God. It's what makes us truly human. Beyond putting others first, it requires sacrificing to help others live. Altruism keeps us going as a species and ensures our species continues to be fruitful and multiply.

People develop altruism by putting love in practice, not just talking about it. Practice includes children playing altruistic roles in the creative play of their own making. Often such play is inspired by real-life events that children experienced or witnessed on the screen, heard through oral tales, or read in books. It results in feeling inspired by people doing their best to make good happen in order to conquer evil.

I grew up reading and longing to be like female heroines such as Florence Nightingale, Harriet Tubman, Clara Barton, and Joan of Arc. As I got older, I was drawn to the courageous altruism of Mother Teresa. Children, and especially traumatized children, must have prototypes, modern heroes or heroines, and archetypes (heroes or heroines from myths or legends) with whom they identify and for whom they have respect. Who we meditate on (or focus on), we become.

Focusing on unhealthy TV programs or movies, and participating in violent computer games doesn't help develop courageous, altruistic character. Focusing on or playing the part of the "bad guy" who hurts innocent living creatures is negative brain training that also doesn't help calm arousal in the lower, reactive part of the brain.

Building courageous altruism and common sense thinking through live observance of heroism

A childhood event made a permanent imprint on my character. It occurred during the 1960s in a small town in a state that was one of the worst human rights violators of the era. White people blatantly suppressed and oppressed African Americans. Their public hatefulness and abuse were tolerated. White people who overtly objected to the local mistreatment of African Americans risked their own safety, as retaliation could be swift and severe.

My beloved aunt (introduced in Chapter 4) didn't care. She believed all people had value in the eyes of God, and demonstrated, from a place deep within her that all children, regardless of color, had a special place in God's heart. She never preached her belief system to me; she didn't have to. She showed me one day at the general store.

As my little sister, my aunt, and I waited in line to pay for items, a little African American boy kept getting in line, like he was supposed to, to pay for his candy. The white shopkeeper kept shooing him away, allowing the white people (who, except for us, were all men) to get in front of him to pay for their items. Eventually the man behind the cash register wouldn't even let him get in the line. The little boy continued to stand by the register holding out the few coins he had in one hand and the meager candy he had in the other. He just wanted to pay.

I watched my aunt in front of me observe what was happening to the child. Although I could only see her back, I could see her bristle and become taller and straighter every time the little boy was rudely shooed away by the man behind the counter.

Silently, resolutely, my aunt began to tap one foot, then the other. Then she placed her hands on her hips, pulled her shoulders back and raised her head higher. She was getting ready. Something was going to happen by the time we reached the counter.

It did. She put her hands on the little boy's shoulders, gently pulled him in front of her, and faced him toward the counter. With one hand still on his shoulder, she leaned over the top of the little guy's head and wagged her index finger quite close to the shop keeper's face. "Now, you take this little boy's money for his candy," she said. "He's been waiting here long enough." To my surprise, the shopkeeper did just as he was told. The little boy paid and went on his way.

That event cemented it for me. My aunt was my hero. I wanted to be just like her.

Overcoming fear to build courageous altruism and common sense thinking through creative play

The Zombie Apocalypse

During school recess, eight-year-old Tevin loved playing an updated version of Tag or Chase that the kids called The Zombie Apocalypse. In this new version, "It" (the one who chased the others in order to tag them) was a zombie. The ones who got tagged would have to join the lead zombie to tag the others still left in the game. The last one tagged got to be the lead zombie in the next round.

I found it interesting that Tevin, in his new school at his new foster-adopt placement, chose this escape-from-danger game instead of the other no-tech movement/social interaction games already going on during recess. He was more interested in "The Zombie Apocalypse" than he was in the other competitive games such as the various team sports games that most of the other kids were playing. He chose the creative, imaginative play. I knew the unconscious, traumatized part of his brain needed this type of play. I knew he was smart enough and resilient enough, in spite of what he had been through before placement, to psychologically benefit from this type of play.

It soon became clear why Tevin needed to play The Zombie Apocalypse. He needed to gain power, through constructive play, over something that frightened him very much.

He disclosed to me and his foster-to-adopt parents that he was afraid the devil could get him. Too afraid to even identify him as the devil, Tevin referred to him as "D." The Zombie Apocalypse game helped him conquer his fear and insecurity that the devil could indeed snatch him. In the game, he had the power to run and escape from "It." It helped that he was athletic and probably faster than many children his age. Every time he played the game he proved to himself how easily he could evade what he feared most.

Tevin liked his new "permanent parents," and they liked him. He was still learning to trust that they were indeed strong enough to take care of him and keep him safe, so that he didn't have to keep himself safe. As he began growing in the security that they might stick around and not get rid of him, he gradually disclosed some of the things that really scared him at night and that made it hard for him to sleep. He talked about the scary movies he had seen when he was in regular foster care.

Prior to his current foster-to-adopt placement, Tevin had lived in a group home for boys. The foster care provider allowed the boys to watch scary movies such as the Jason and Freddie Krueger films. The movie that scared Tevin the most was *The Conjuring* (2013), a horrifying movie of demonic possession, mothers killing their babies, and a family being persecuted, for no reason, by evil incarnate.

So Tevin developed a fear of the devil and had trouble sleeping. He was removed from an abusive, dangerous, frightening birth home by Texas Children's Protective Services to be placed in a dangerous, abusive, frightening group foster home.

The non-thinking, reactive part of the brain cannot tell the difference between fact and fiction via the television set or any other two-dimensional screen for that matter, be it computer or cell phone. Violence and fear conveyed through an electronic medium assaults the brain in the same way it would if the person personally witnessed or experienced the harm and havoc.

Tevin had been retraumatized and re-assaulted in foster care, but now his perpetrator was Satan. At least when his perpetrators were human, as in the birth home, he had some sense of predictability about when the people who were supposed to be caring for him were dangerous. If he smelled alcohol—run! If he saw someone moving through the house in a threatening manner—hide! But Satan and his demons? How do you hide from something that is omnipotent and omnipresent, in a really diabolical way?

His foster-adopt parents and I had to help this precious and innocent child. We helped Tevin apply the courageous skills he developed to escape from the zombie in the playground chase game to a new game, and gently pushed him a little farther into even more resilience. In the new game using little miniature figures, his new parents and I joined and supported Jedi knight freedom fighter, Commander Tevin, in his courageous, altruistic, successful "fight" to defeat the evil "D." Finally, he wouldn't have to fight alone.

With the therapist (me) as coach, the foster-adopt parents and Tevin began the healing creative play. I picked from the available miniature figures the most innocuous, benign little devil figure. He actually looked more like the little Hot Stuff character from the days of Casper the Friendly Ghost. Yes, I, the therapist, picked the "D." I wanted to show Tevin that the figure I chose to represent the one he was most afraid of, was no bigger than about 2½ inches tall, with a baby belly, and a silly little pout on his face when he didn't get his way: nothing to be frightened of. Tevin was definitely bigger.

On his own, Tevin selected the rest of his support team: three angels, and not one but two Jesuses. He wanted to be doubly protected. He picked an average looking boy to represent himself.

His parents chose strong, protective, superhero-like figures to represent themselves.

Next Tevin picked the defensive weapons he would use to defeat the "D" in battle after battle. (Children have to play it out over and over again for their brain to get some form of resolution regarding the matter that is causing them discomfort.)

It is important that children have opportunities to use their imagination and select play items to symbolize what they want to portray in play. Their "pretend" items better help the smart part of their brains develop abstract thinking. Abstract thinking is a goal of the mature smart part of the brain. In play situations, this means being able to imagine beyond the concrete, visible object that one can see and use logic and common sense to locate another item that represents the real item. When children can use their imagination and "pretend" that certain items on hand represent what they need in their play, they are using their ability to create from scratch. When children create the seen from the unseen, it helps make the smart part of their brain even smarter because they become better problem solvers. So, Tevin found all types of things in my office that he could turn into defensive weapons against "D": rubber bands, hollow plastic Easter eggs, pens, scotch tape, plastic knives, a hole punch, and marbles. He distributed the items to his army.

I moved the benign little "D" character, but only as directed by Tevin. He needed to be the one in control in this situation since it was his fear, not mine; however, it was my responsibility, as a protective elder, to minimize the power of the pathetic little creature. So, I made sure that "D" was a sniveling little coward who was all comic-like bark and no bite.

Quickly, Tevin was ready to take the lead, be benevolently courageous, and win in the end. The parents' role was to support Commander Tevin as active members of his defense force. At first, what structure I offered was for the parents. In order to support Tevin and not take over the play, nor traumatize him further, they needed guidance in using support methods and understanding the healing power of positive play.

As Tevin and his team defeated "D" in battle after battle, he got braver, more confident, and more creative in his battle strategies. Interestingly enough, as he gained more confidence and defeated his own fear of the devil, he became more thoughtful of his army of parents. A good commander looks out for his soldiers. Because he had less fear with each successful battle, he had more energy to put toward the survival of others, instead of the survival of just himself, and it showed as his play progressed.

At first, Tevin wanted the little devil to be a silent retreater when he and his army drove him off with an arsenal of volleyed marbles, paper clips, plastic knives (spears of course), and rubber bands that sling-shot hollow Easter eggs. He and his soldiers did an amazing job of providing the necessary sound effects of a conquering army.

Of course, as the successful good guy battles raged on, Tevin allowed the enemy to gradually have more of a voice. I made sure that voice was of a big baby bully who yelped as he ran away in fear and defeat. Tevin needed that control. He needed to be bigger than his fear. And his fear was not just the horrific scenes of the horror movie that were lodged in his conscious and subconscious, but also of the accompanying creepy, terrifying movie sound track. He didn't want the devil to say anything at first because he feared it would be the warning sounds of impending death and torment of the terrified human beings in the movie who could do nothing to save themselves.

After fighting and winning subsequent battles, Tevin grew in confidence and he wanted "D" to say certain things, like "I'm gonna get you; you'll never see me sneaking up on you." But of course, Tevin did see him, every time. The "D" not only failed to surprise and hurt Tevin and company time and time again, but he also got a walloping in the process.

I made "D" obey Tevin. I made "D's" futile attempts to defeat the good guys exceptionally silly and had him flee from them in sniveling, cowardly retreat, over and over again. I knew if I could get Tevin laughing at how silly "D" behaved and what a poor loser he was, then Tevin would be further encouraged and empowered. If I had decided when and how to move the "D" and made him as scary as he really had been to Tevin, then Tevin could have been further traumatized.

Through this process, I reframed Tevin's emotional experience of the horror movie *The Conjuring*. Because he watched that movie, he became a helpless participant of the horror portrayed on the screen, just like those who the movie depicted. Now Tevin's brain could begin to have a different experience. Hopefully, if he continued to play some version of "Tevin beats the D" at home and at school, then "Tevin beats the D" will be the emotional experience that imprints on his brain rather than the visual images and emotional horror that were implanted by that movie.

At the end of the game, "D" was captured and put in jail. Jail was an upside-down box that the parents sat on top of as they held the miniatures of the two Jesuses and the angels, so that the captive enemy had no chance of escape. When it was time for the game to end, it was important to visually lock the image in for Tevin that "D" could not get out unless Tevin wanted him to. Also, it was important that Tevin get the concrete visual image of his parents along with those above us who are the most powerful, protecting him from harm and keeping the devil in his rightful place—locked up with no place to go.

For creative play to be healing for the brain and the soul, good must win in the end, and the hurting child must be the "good." To learn that they are not fighting their battles alone, and that they can depend on their caregivers to help them, not hurt them, children must practice through play—with their protecting parents.

Our goal was to help Tevin enjoy the creative, imaginative play so much he would want to repeat the play, not just in this session, but at home as well. We also hoped that, eventually, Tevin would continue the play theme on his own, as much as he needed to, for his brain to make the necessary shift in thinking that there really were adults who cared enough about him to fight for him.

Children should get healthy enough to structure and enact their own play without necessary support from the healthier caregivers. They have to have practice in their own creative problem-solving. They have to have practice in overcoming and in resilience, by their own accord, not by someone else's.

Imaginative play should be productive. Hurting children should not be allowed to retraumatize themselves or have other people retraumatize them with violent play or visual images. They shouldn't be allowed to stay stuck in a post-traumatic, self-defeating destructive play cycle, like an endless violent computer game where evil triumphs. When children can have free reign in their creative, imaginative play because their play is healing, they are on the path to recovery. Non-directed play can then be a method of self-help.

Before the popularity of ultra-violence and terror via TV, movies, and electronic gaming, children's play could be less monitored and guided by caring, healthy adults. In my day, we were just told to go outside and play. We did, for hours. That play was psychologically constructive, even for the children for whom their home was a hurting, scary place. But times were different then. Due to the lack of electronic devices and TV stations, if we didn't want to be bored to death, we played. What we did have to watch on TV was relatively benign. Good won over not-so-scary badness—always. Altruism and courage reigned on the television set. And that's what our creative, imaginative play reflected. Nowadays, adults need to have more of an active hand in building resilience in the traumatized children they care for.

Abuse survival as boot camp training for higher-level thinking

Good cause–effect thinking is a complex function of the smart part of the brain. It requires sufficient interhemispheric integration or communication of the two sides (hemispheres) of the smart part of the brain—and intelligence-driven common sense. For a person to identify the correct potential events caused by certain actions, that person needs some common sense in part developed from prior experience in "real-world" problem-solving.

Here's an example of poor higher-level thinking: if someone has never driven a car or even a four-wheeled vehicle, then that person really shouldn't take a driving test to get a driver's license. The person will likely fail the test (effect) because the person doesn't know how to drive (cause). It doesn't matter that the person has been in a car numerous times, can drive a car on a computer screen, and thinks "real-world" driving looks easy.

So, for example, when a young man who has never driven before fails a driving test, he should at least realize he failed because he had no driving experience in a real vehicle. The young man should have the common sense to learn how to actually drive before taking the test again instead of retaking the test until by magic he passes, or the examiner rewards him with a license just to get rid of him.

The preceding story actually happened. The young man could neither figure out why he kept failing the driving test, nor identify the most important effect of not knowing how to drive:

If I don't know how to drive and I get in a car and start driving, then I am a potential danger to myself and others.

Cause: I don't know how to drive.

Effect: I endanger myself and others when I am behind the wheel.

Instead his cause–effect thinking was not only faulty, but also reversed:

Effect: I can drive.

Cause: If I get a driver's license.

His thinking went no further than that.

When younger, did he not have enough problem-solving play or activities or real-world experiences in thinking? No, he did not. He was 20 years old at the time of the above event, and he had been raised on video/computer games and TV shows that provided entertainment and action, but little else. He also had *not* had a lot of opportunity to observe his parents making and carrying out well-thought out problem-solving activities because they didn't. His parents weren't abusive, they just didn't teach him anything that was useful for adulthood.

If an abused child of at least average intelligence has made it out of hell on earth and is still alive, that child should have developed some higher thinking skills. The child should be able to put some "cause" to the "effect." There should be some "street smarts" or common sense thinking going on in the smart part of the brain.

If abused children received at least some care and nurturing some of the time when they were infants, then their brains may have received enough preparedness for higher level thinking, (i.e., if I cry, I make something happen). Of course, with a nurturer, the child's needs are met; with an abuser, the child is punished.

A child's ability to learn to "connect the dots" for survival's sake gets developed whether the child is with an abuser or with a nurturer. "If I cry with this person or even if I am seen by that person, I could be in danger." The child with better emotional regulation and impulse control acts accordingly, making the right choices such as being silent or being invisible in order to avoid pain.

Cause: If I cry.

Effect: I might get hurt.

Smart common sense solution: I don't cry.

Smart thinking being developed: Don't trust that people will take care of my needs.

If that same abused child also repetitively played no-tech, constructive, creative play with other children as an outlet, then that child may be better able to "real-world" out-common sense think a child from a non-abusive home who grew up, instead, being raised by the TV and by the computer—because the latter child experienced neglect. Instead of helping the brain develop, neglect causes it to become stagnant.

Is overreliance on technology hampering higher-level thinking skills, courage, and altruism?

People don't read like they used to. People don't think and problem-solve like they used to, either. As reading for pleasure has decreased, and reliance on technology has increased, the ability of our young people to think deeply and use the imagination has also decreased.

Screens do not necessarily provide real, live training in courage and altruism, either. But real live experiences of witnessing others, with whom one has a relationship, performing acts of courage and altruism do. And so does imaginative, pretend play when those virtues are practiced with the physical body, not just the computer mouse.

At least when children can spend some time (not all day) viewing courageous altruism on screen or becoming an on-screen hero who risks her life so others can be safe via an altruistic computer game, those visual experiences could be helpful—if they are also practiced in the real world. When play reflects what is experienced on screen, and is played out in the physical body, it can become a part of one's automatic reaction. But if the person doesn't transfer that courageous altruism from the screen to the body via real-life experiences or play experiences, how can it stick? The person has only practiced what to do when heroism is virtual, not real-life necessary. It's just not the same medium of experience.

In computer gaming, much of what children view or play on a screen is predominantly real-time action shown as it is happening. This does not allow the smart part of the brain time to reflect, analyze, or imagine. Viewing "on-screen" action in progress does not help the smart part of the brain sustain attention for long enough periods of time to deeply think about the information conveyed, nor the potential ramifications of that information.

After analyzing more than 50 studies on learning and technology including research on multi-tasking and the use of computers, the Internet and video games, Patricia Greenfield (2009) found that as technology became more important in people's lives, skills in higher level or critical thinking and analysis declined.

For people to function in the real world, they need to spend most of their time in the real world. Children, especially hurting children, need to spend most of their time moving and interacting in the real world with real others instead of sitting on their behinds watching television or interacting with something that someone else created for them on a screen.

Real-world play, games, and activities to better sharpen the smart part of the brain

Interhemispheric communication or integration (when the smart part of the brain is the effective command central for brain and body) is the result of successful differentiation (when the brain becomes more organized into specialized centers). Interhemispheric communication is necessary for people to do their best higher thinking and override impulses coming from the more reactive non-thinking parts of the lower brain.

An adequate sense of body-in-space or proprioception helps support the smart part of the brain. A good sense of proprioception can help the smart part of the brain stay on line. It can help someone stay present and not go floating off into the wild, blue yonder. Hence, all the games and the activities in this section utilize the prerequisite brain skills which enable the smart part of the brain to be successful. These prerequisite brain skills continue to become sharper which, in turn, continues the development of the smart part of the brain.

Parlor games and activities...or fun ways children can entertain themselves and be entertained when they can't go outside

Charades

This game is not for the extremely socially anxious as players are required to stand up in front of others and silently act out words or phrases that teammates try to guess. The person who guesses what is being acted out gets the next turn.

For the game to be fun, it should be kept at the developmental level of the players. For example, maybe children can act out animals or people with whom everyone present is familiar. Others may act out common actions that would be fairly easy to figure out, like rowing a boat, swimming, or vacuuming the floor. Because the actor can't make sounds or mouth words, their entire effort is based on creative, physical body expression.

Charades requires actors to exercise flexibility and attune themselves to the audience's needs. If the audience doesn't understand what the action of the actor means, then the actor should try something else, not keep doing the same thing. Charades is a good exercise in making an effort to connect with others and try different methods to help others understand what the actor wants to convey. It's good communication practice that requires putting others first. The actor has to work to be understood. It also helps develop common sense thinking in all the players as it helps children practice using their memory, their imagination, and their past experiences.

Spoons: A card game

This fast-moving game requires alertness, sustained attention, and multi-tasking, all smart part of the brain skills. Socio-emotionally, it connects people face to face in a fun and silly way which reduces social anxiety and encourages people to enjoy each other and themselves in the company of others.

It is played with a simple deck of cards, kitchen spoons, and at least four people. There should be enough spoons for all the people playing, minus one.

Players sit around a table. The dealer deals each player four cards and places the deck, and the spoons, in the middle of the table. Players look at their own cards and, as the game commences, tries to get all four of any card. The dealer selects a card from the top of the deck and rapidly passes one card from his hand that he doesn't want to the person on his left. That player, following the pace of the dealer, does the same thing to the person on his left. The last player puts an unwanted card into a discard pile. If the cards from the deck run out, then the discard pile can be reshuffled and used.

The first player to get four of a kind sneakily pulls a spoon from the center of the circle and continues to pass cards as if nothing happened. The other players catch on and start doing likewise, quietly pulling a spoon from the center as they continue to pass cards as though nothing ever happened.

Eventually, the one person left without a spoon loses that round. The consequence for losing depends on the number of people playing. With fewer players, the goal can be to avoid spelling out the word "spoon." The first time a person loses a round, that's an "s." The next time the person loses a round, that's a "p."

Another version of this game is called "Pig." Instead of using spoons, the first person to get four of a kind puts a finger to her nose. It is difficult to continue passing cards and holding one's finger on the nose. Fairly good differentiation of body parts is necessary for this version or cards will be flying everywhere!

Storytelling

As reading is on the decline, so is aural (listening) comprehension, aural memory, and the ability to sustain attention when information is conveyed verbally instead of through visual or written means.

Good storytellers engage and connect with their audiences. Verbally, they paint visual pictures for their listeners with physical body movements, sound effects, facial expressions, and background information inserted at just the right time. They draw listeners' rapt attention and subtly urge them to use their higher thinking capabilities. By unfolding tales as they are happening, in the sequential order of occurrence as if one is there, storytellers help listeners better sequence their thoughts and visual images which later on can help them verbally relate events in a logical, sequential, organized fashion.

Children should be discouraged from interrupting the storyteller with questions. That practice hones impulse control and listening skills.

My paternal grandmother was an incredible storyteller. She lived much of her life in the country with no electricity or phone. She took up the tradition of passing on oral histories. After supper on the front porch, while mending or shelling peas, my grandmother spun yarns of life in the South Mississippi farming community known as Cracker's Neck.

Her mind was clear and sharp. Her memories were vivid. Sitting at her feet enrapt, I felt as if I were there with her as she depicted the events from times before even she had been born. She included pictorial details in her stories that a mind needed in order to join her in shared visual imagery. She included such details as how hot it was, or where the menfolk were at the time something happened.

She would set the scene by describing old folks sitting on the front porch of the ancestral home in Cracker's Neck, rocking in their rocking chairs. Then she would shock us describing the sudden appearance of a sick, dangerous, rabid dog. I saw people narrowly escaping as if I were there. I could envision grandmothers firing out of their seats, shooting past the opened screen door and into the house for safety. I could imagine a foaming, snarling, old flea-bitten mongrel not knowing where or who he was, but still moving forward, menacingly, toward the folks who had been on that porch. I could hear the empty, still-rocking rocking chairs as that old confused, sick dog meandered past where the people had been sitting.

Was that how the situation really played out? It didn't matter. What I saw in my imagination led me to reflect on the story and ask questions, to myself and to my grandmother (when she finished the story), so that I could deeply ponder the matter.

The story also inspired me to make preliminary plans for what I would do, just in case a mad dog caught me off guard wherever I was. I mentally rehearsed how fast I would move and what I would do to reach safety: planned cause–effect thinking and resiliency practice.

Button, Button, Who's Got the Button?

Several players sit around in a circle with their hands in their laps in prayer position with the thumbs and fingers pointed horizontally. Another player who is apart from the seated group, the passer, has a small object hidden inside his equally prayer-positioned hands. He walks around the inside of the circle pretending to insert the small object (stone, paper clip, or actual button) into each prayer-posed player's receiving hands. Here's the catch: the passer will actually place the object into one player's hands, and both will give no clue that it transpired. Their facial expressions won't change. Being effectively sneaky is the goal! They will exercise emotional regulation and impulse control.

Players begin guessing who could be holding the object. They must exercise planned cause–effect thinking and common sense while looking for clues. They study the mannerisms, facial expressions and attitudes of the other players. Who is slightly smirking? Whose eyes could be twinkling? Who could be acting a little more nervous? With whom did the walker spend a little too much time? Good social observations can pay off and become refined with practice.

The players must feel fairly sure they know who is hiding the object before they start blurting out the names of the suspects (impulse control). The one who guesses correctly gets to be the next passer.

Chess

I described in Chapter 6 the benefits I got from this game as a child. Primarily, it helped me cognitively override threat in order to make good decisions and control impulses.

Chess is an intense game of planned cause–effect thinking, common sense problem-solving, emotional regulation, and impulse control. It is too complex to describe how to play chess in this section but numerous explanations can be found on the Internet and on the instructions that accompany an actual chess game.

I was probably taught by my father to play chess at too early of an age. Most children can better enjoy the game and glean benefits from it when they are older, probably no younger than age 10 or 11. A child has to have some ability to reason and strategize for this game to help increase their thinking skills rather than confuse them. Here's a good test to see if a child is ready to start learning how to play chess:

See if a child can successfully answer this question: Is it closer to New Orleans by train or by bus? Children who reason, "Neither, it's the same distance regardless of how you get there" are ready for chess. Children who answer, "train" or "bus" or "I don't know" would be better served learning checkers or Monopoly first. On the other hand, maybe a child could come up with the correct answer to the "by train or by bus" question by learning to play chess.

Chinese Checkers

The exact directions for Chinese Checkers come with the game or can be found on the Internet. Played by 2 to 6 people on a board that forms a six-pointed star, the game requires each player to move a set number of marbles from one point of the star to the opposite point of the star.

As a child, I liked this game because of the marbles. Their weight gave me proprioceptive input and helped ground me. I found it to be a much simpler and less intimidating game than chess with fewer and easier rules. It is a nice prerequisite to chess because Chinese Checkers requires strategy, impulse control, patience while waiting for others to plan their moves, and planned cause–effect thinking.

Scavenger Hunts

In a scavenger hunt, pairs of children compete to be the first to find objects hidden by the creator of the hunt. That creator provides written clues that describe the object and its location. The game requires at least four players. It can vary in level of difficulty and be played indoors or out.

For an indoor hunt, objects could be everyday items common to any home, such as a roll of toilet paper, scissors, or a sponge. A simple hunt offer clues like this: "The sponge is in a room used for sleep. It is hidden under something that people put their head on at night." If children aren't able to read well or at all, someone can read the clues for them. In such instances, children practice their listening skills along with their sequencing skills and logical thinking.

Scavenger hunts are fun, paired thinking and moving games that include a good dose of face-to-face socialization practice. A scavenger hunt gets pairs of kids talking with each other and working together to follow the written or verbal directions that will lead them to find items on a list. To succeed, children must control or cognitively override their excitement to identify the items first, carefully read or listen to the locating clues for meaning, talk about it, think about it, and then go after the described items after careful contemplation—and be the first pair to do so.

I Spy

This guessing game requires no props or accessories, just children and an item to be identified according to verbal clues given by the "spy." Because it can be created spontaneously, it's great to play in a pinch—at home, in a waiting area, in a vehicle stuck in traffic. It's good for anywhere one has bored, about-to-start squabbling kids.

The designated spy spots an item to be identified by the others and is careful not to be caught looking at it (self-awareness practice). The spy also has to be careful of personal body language, so that hands and arms aren't flailing about (self-control) giving visual clues about the item being described by indicating its size, shape, and location.

Children have to visualize the object as they are either describing it or picturing it as it is described. That in itself is a task that requires effective communication of both hemispheres of the smart part of the brain and certainly gives children practice in accessing both hemispheres quickly.

The spy gives one clue, such as the color, size, or use for the object. If the guessers are unable to identify the object by the first clue that is given, the spy continues to give clues one at a time until someone identifies the object correctly. The winner gets to be the next spy.

Children should be discouraged from impulsively blurting out answers that don't fit the clue. Getting to be the next spy is a just reward for the careful, contemplative thinker who actually listens to the spy and uses the spoken clues to locate the item.

The Hot/Cold Game

In this game, all the players but one leave the room. The remaining person hides an object for the players to find. The players already know what object they must search for when they return. The object must be small, so it is not readily spotted. When the hider of the object is ready for the others to return to begin the search for the item, the person invites the searchers back in by calling "Ready!"

The only clues the searchers receive are expressions that indicate, according to temperature, how close one is to the hidden item. The farther from the object, the colder a player is. The closer, the hotter. To indicate a player is moving farther from the object, the caller might say, "You're cold…cold…colder…freezing." When a player is approaching the object, the hider can elevate the excitement through word choice and vocal inflection. "You're getting warmer. warrrrrmer…now you're hot… Hot! … Oh, you're burning!"

The caller can help the searchers navigate. If a player is heading in the right direction, but turns, the hider might quickly change from "hot" to "Uh-oh, you're getting colder again."

In this game, the caller wants someone to find the object, so he should be helpful and compassionate. It's a nice, cooperative game that reduces threat so searchers can be better focused and motivated to find the object.

The game helps smart part brain development in different ways. First, the caller has to practice self-awareness by controlling facial expressions and body language that would give clues as to where the object is. The searcher learns to better read body language to notice if the caller could be unconsciously indicating the location of the item.

The children seeking the item have to sustain their focus on the verbal clues that the caller gives and abstract the possibilities of where the object could logically be—not run around willy-nilly flipping everything over because their hands and fingers can do so. The game aids impulse control and brain organization (differentiation).

The verbal clues help children use their brain to direct the movement of their bodies toward a goal: the hidden object. The verbal clues also help children who are directionally impaired (proprioception) but improving, to better process language and understand that words or expressions of heat or coldness indicate that that the body is to move in a certain direction. Children with significant proprioceptive deficits and language processing problems may find this game too developmentally challenging.

Escape from danger or keep-from-getting-caught games
Hide and Go Seek

Hide and Go Seek is a simple, relatively benign "keep from getting caught" game that has been around forever and is common in cultures around the world. To start the game, the seeker covers her eyes and, in a 60-beat-a-minute rhythm, counts to a number high enough to give the other players time to scatter and hide. Enough time should be allotted for the bigger kids to help the smaller kids hide. In a real emergency, it is not every man for himself, but the survival of the group that is important. When the seeker finishes counting, she opens her eyes and announces "Ready or not, here I come!," and searches for the hiding players. The last one she finds and subsequently tags becomes the seeker in the next round.

During the game, children who practice impulse control and are able to refrain from wiggling or making noise for what seems like forever sometimes are rewarded by being the last person found. Children have to exercise lots of quick, higher thinking to find the best hiding places. They have to learn that the most obvious hiding places will be the first ones searched.

It's a fun game with many variations. Some versions include chase or tag. When one gets spotted, the hider has a chance to run to a designated base before being touched or tagged by the seeker. This is a good survival skill. It's good to choose a hiding place where one can make a fast exit if necessary.

Hide and Go Seek may have originated during dangerous, primitive times when parents had to teach their young to hide from danger, and children practiced hiding while not stirring nor making a sound until it was safe to come out. The game may have evolved from a need to ensure the survival of the young so the tribe or group could continue.

When a skill is practiced that can be utilized in dangerous times for one's survival, the same emotional state of alertness and relative calmness that was present during play may be carried over to the real event. In such actual incidents, if running or fighting won't work, successfully hiding from danger is a necessary survival skill. Children must learn it when they are young so it becomes part of their automatic response and practiced kinesthetic memory.

How many parents have to leave their older children at home alone and want them to exercise good, common sense and get to safety if someone were to come to the house who could harm them? Perhaps think of turning the safety plan into a fun game of Hide and Go Seek.

Escape from the Bubbling Bacteria

My friends and I created this outdoor game in the early to mid-1960s. When someone was washing his car and soap suds ran down the driveway and into the gutters along the side of the street, we children rode our bicycles through the bubbling mess, pretending the suds were dangerous, radioactive bacteria.

During play, we children had to remember to lift our feet off the pedals and keep our legs high in the air as we rode through the soap suds, as any bubbles touching the skin constituted being infected. To successfully escape contamination, we had to learn to modulate the speed of our bicycles to get through the soap suds without incident. The smart part of our brains practiced being in charge of forward momentum. The consequences for an overly exuberant, dysregulated kid stuck on "go" could be disastrous—not only for that child but for the others who could be endangered by non-thinking actions.

When we played as children, everyone sought individual and group success. We operated as a team against the enemy soap suds. We looked out for one another, courageously and altruistically. The more experienced kids even gave riding tips to the lesser experienced.

Kids quickly learned, either by their own experience or by someone else's example, that it behooved them to ride close behind the rider in front of them, without the wheels of their bikes touching. Riding close but not too close behind another rider decreased the sloshing of the soap-sud waves for the second rider because the water was still somewhat parted for the second bicycle. If one or both of the consecutive riders were careless, then a bike crash could cause at least one person to be engulfed in the poisonous concoction. No one wanted that.

The heart-pumping fun this game engendered helped me, and probably others, have hope and courage in conquering our own fears and in overcoming obstacles in our lives at that time, but there was a future payoff: when driving my car, I never got stuck in high water when local roads would flash flood due to the torrential rains. I believe that was because I got extra training in wet-roadway cause–effect thinking as a kid on a bicycle escaping the bubbling bacteria.

Ain't No Boogers Out Tonight

This escape-from-danger game can only be played after dark and should be limited in area to about a single backyard. First, the designated booger hides somewhere from which she can later leap and chase the other players. As the booger watches from her hiding place, the other children walk together, en masse, holding each other for safety, and watching for the sudden emergence of the booger while repeatedly chanting:

Ain't no boogers out tonight

Grandpa killed 'em all last night.

When the booger sees the cluster getting close to her, she jumps out and rushes toward the group while making fierce, threatening sounds. Children scream and scatter in all directions, each player searching for a place to hide because there is no safe base in this game.

The booger chases kids until each gets caught. The last person caught becomes the next booger.

When we played as children, bigger kids altruistically protected the smaller kids because, of course, the booger would know she would easily catch the smaller, slower-moving children. Sometimes before play, we even planned who would help whom to better ensure the younger kids' safety. Often I acted as decoy and detour for my little sister. During the chase, bigger kids might taunt the booger to get her to chase them while someone else helped the little ones hide. It was good practice in altruism and in taking care of the smaller others first.

The kids who were the most successful in evading the booger not only had already mentally multi-tasked the prospective escape routes and best hiding places for themselves, but also had intelligently speculated the best booger hiding places as well. We learned we could be prepared and think ahead. Also, mental rehearsal of what to do when the booger jumped out lessened the likelihood of a freeze response. We had already practiced "action" in our minds before it happened, so our bodies just followed through on what our brains had already practiced.

This game wasn't retraumatizing for those of us who came from a hurting place. When someone was caught, nothing bad happened. Little ones were protected by the bigger ones. No one was in it alone. Walking and chanting and acting in unison, children can feel more confident and less alone. Also, no one was forced to play. Anyone could watch us play or go do something else. I'm sure that the kids who needed to play this game for their own emotional well-being joined in.

This game, and the play practice of other escape-from-danger running games, was very likely good training for me as I grew older and found myself in situations of emergency when it was necessary to run from such dangers as escaping from a fire or moving out of the path of an oncoming vehicle. These games might also have given my brain and body training to act altruistically to help save someone's life. I think they did.

Music training and physical activities
Piano, drumming, guitar, and other types of musical instrument activities

Serious instrument playing (instead of just banging around to create noise) is excellent for helping children coordinate both sides of their brain. Certainly, the individual, yet coordinated movements of the fingers and perhaps hands needed to make the music helps to better organize the brain (differentiation). Also, when children practice keeping time to the music, their brains practice better rhythm which helps brain control. This activity also increases children's ability to better synchronize rhythmically with others in social situations.

Bike riding

Bike riding helps children use arms and legs in a coordinated, rhythmically timed manner which exercises both sides of the brain simultaneously because of the alternate movement of the legs. Furthermore, keeping the upper body erect with the hands on the handlebars as the legs move helps the brain achieve differentiation as the circuitry between the two hemispheres of the brain is strengthened by the alternate movement of the legs. In bicycling, the top part of the body is differentiated from the bottom part: top part still, bottom part moving.

For children to maintain balance on a bicycle, their brain must practice directing the body to maintain balance from the midline of the body; hence, both hands on the handlebars, one each side, helps the body to feel that balance when the weight is distributed equally on either side of the handlebars.

Bike riding also increases kinesthetic, or muscle, memory. Disorganized children with differentiation delays often have problems with kinesthetic memory. In bike riding, the brain directs body parts to do what they are supposed to in a coordinated, timely manner faster and faster each time the activity is practiced. With practice, children may add more tasks while bike riding, such as talking or singing (while looking out for accidents before they happen, of course). Manual scooters, tricycles, and bikes with training wheels are good upright prerequisites to two-wheeled bike riding.

Swimming

Learning to swim (not just float and splash) and practicing that skill can be a good prerequisite to riding a two-wheeled bike. For one, swimming doesn't require balance because the water supports the body. The water through which the body learns to travel provides proprioceptive feedback that the lower reaches of the brain enjoy.

This activity forces the body to coordinate head, upper body, and lower body so it can stay afloat and go somewhere. The brain gets practice directing the body to separate body parts and move them in a complimentary fashion to propel it forward. Swimming provides the similar coordinated, rhythmic bilateral brain stimulation that the executive functioning or smart part of the brain needs to come on line effectively.

Attachment between caregiving adults and their children can also be facilitated when adults are in the water with the children, helping them learn to swim. Children can lose their fear of the water when protective adults teach them to float on their backs by way of supportive adult hands under their bodies that won't let them go until they are ready to float on their own.

Sports and other organized physical activities

If children show some athletic leanings, then by all means get them involved in organized sports. For children whose bodies and brains just aren't ready to compete with agile others on a field, organized physical games that allow them to go at their own pace are less stressful and, hopefully, more fun.

CROQUET

Children who have matured to a point where they are ready to practice extending their concentration and patience may enjoy croquet. It exercises alertness and focus, and provides brain-telling-body-what-to-do practice when they use hand-held mallets to hit wooden balls through hoops. The vibration coursing through the upper body joints when children strike the heavy wooden balls provides proprioceptive feedback that feels good and orients the brain to where the body is in time and in space.

PADDLE BALL

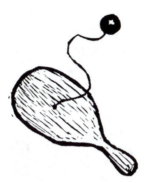

Figure 7.1 Paddle ball

For fast-moving, highly anxious, dysregulated children, playing paddle ball (Figure 7.1) can feel as fun and ultimately calming as jumping on the pogo stick.

Children have to learn to follow the ball. Their brains have to practice anticipating where the ball might go after it rhythmically and rapidly bounces against the hard wooden (or plastic) paddle. Whenever the ball on its strong elastic string crosses the midline of a child's body, the child's hand, arm, eyes, and attention have to do the same.

The slapping sound and vibration the ball makes every time it hits the paddle activates children's joints proprioceptively. The activity helps children practice focus, concentration, and more rapid interhemispheric switching as they start, stop, readjust their body in space, and make rapid physical transition in pursuit of the bouncing ball. Children can get even more consistent, repetitive practice by competing with themselves or with another to see how many consecutive times they can paddle the ball without missing.

Rhythmic play with a purpose

THIS A-WAY VALERIE (OR STRUT MISS SUZIE)

Oh, did we girls love this partnered line-dancing game. As I've taught it over the years with groups (it does take a fairly large group to play), I discovered that the boys love it, too.

Start by forming two parallel lines and have each participant partner with the person who is directly across. The partners then join hands. When the rhythmic singing starts, partners bounce-dance with each other in an arms-and-legs-synchronized fashion (see Figure 7.2). Both partners bounce and extend their arms and legs homo-laterally (same arm and same leg, same side) in a rhythmic seesawing-push-me/pull-you manner. This coordinated effort makes the partnered dancers feel as if they are moving as one unit, contra-lateral to each other.

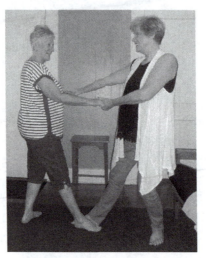

Figure 7.2 Contra-lateral pose

As a person moves in synchronized rhythm to another person's coordinated movements, their brains and social connections get a positive boost. By dancing and holding hands in contra-lateral rhythmic unison (Figure 7.2), couples can jumpstart a budding romance or strengthen a bond that's already there. And what could be more enjoyable and bonding, for parents and children, than parents joyfully holding their children close to them, looking into their eyes, and dancing with them?

In the version of "Strut Miss Suzie" we sang, we emphasized the words that coordinated the contra-lateral movements of our arms and legs and we bounced in rhythm with our partner.

We sang:

This a-way Valerie

That a-way Valerie

This a-way Valerie

All the day long

Facing our partners and holding hands, we bounced once and moved on the first word of each line while jointly moving our arms and legs contra-laterally to each other. Next, we dropped hands, reformed our two separate lines and began clapping and moving rhythmically to the next group of words we sang. At the same time, the first person on either the right or the left at the front of the line began "sassily" walking down through the two adjacent lines of kids to the end of the line to the words of:

Strut Miss Suzie

Strut Miss Suzie

Strut Miss Suzie

All the day long

Then the partner of the child who started the "strutting" would dance or walk "sassily" down the line of kids to the end, while the two lines of children sang and moved rhythmically to:

Here comes another one

Just like the other one

Here comes another one

All the day long

Then the kids would again grasp the hands of their partners and repeat the dance pattern to "This a-way Valerie, that a-way Valerie…" The "Strut Miss Suzie" part and the "Here comes another one" part only changed slightly. This time, the first kid of the next pair of partnered children at the front of the lines got to have his or her real name called while he strutted. And, of course, the second child of the pair who strutted was just "Here comes another one just like the other one." This pattern of partner dancing and strutting continued until the kids just got tired of playing it. It was important, however, that everyone got a turn to strut down the center of the parallel lines.

The benefits, besides the social ones already mentioned, of a partnered line-dancing game are immeasurable for the brain: rhythm enhances the brain, the jumping and clapping are proprioceptively enhancing, the contra-lateral coordination of the partnered movements boosts interhemispheric integration and downcast moods can be positively shifted by the shared pleasure of this game.

Jump rope activities

Compared to today's jump ropes, jump ropes of the past were heavier and had heavier wooden handles, which better supported the sense of proprioception. Children may use a shorter rope to jump alone, or may jump (alone or with others) while two other children twirl the rope for them.

To help facilitate rhythm, children may sing or chant as they jump. One of the most familiar songs of my day was "Cinderella."

> *Cinderella,*
>
> *Dressed in yellow*
>
> *Went upstairs*
>
> *To kiss her fellow*
>
> *Made a mistake*
>
> *And kissed a snake*
>
> *How many doctors*
>
> *Did it take*
>
> *One, two, three…*

and on into infinity or until the jumper tired and got tangled up in the rope.

The "Queen Bee" chant (another old favorite) accompanies a competitive game of chase via jumping rope. One child "runs in" and begins jumping a rope being turned by children on either end. While jumping, she calls for someone watching on the side to "run in" and chase her by chanting:

> *Queen Bee*
>
> *Chase me, _____* (first name of person selected to chase)

The first jumper then attempts to run out before the second jumper runs in. Around and around they go, into the rope, then out of the rope, until someone gets tripped up in the rope or the first person gets apprehended.

In jump rope, even the people turning the ropes are getting a brain workout. Proprioceptively, their joints get to vibrate from the weight of the rope as it hits the ground on its downward journey. The sound and the feel of the rope hitting the ground helps to set the rhythm of the chant and of the jumper's jumping.

The rope turners have to figure out how to turn the rope in a synchronized, cross-midline-of-the-body manner. They have to chant and coordinate the turning of the rope at the same time, in a predictable, rhythmic fashion so the jumper may enter in time to the turning of the rope.

Jumping helps the jumper exercise the on/off switch of the brain (differentiation), jars the joints (proprioceptive input), and gives jumpers practice with rhythmic synchronistic movement in time to the rope and to the chant. This not only helps the smart part of the brain respond faster to designated mental tasks in the real world, but also helps practiced jumpers join with others in social rhythmic synchronicity.

CHAPTER QUESTIONS

1. Escape from danger or keep-from-getting-caught games provide great physical multi-level brain training for children which, if practiced, leads to better thinking in the future when fast thinking and action are called for. What escape from danger or keep-from-getting-caught games do you remember playing as a child, and how do you think you benefitted from playing those games? What physical escape-from-danger or keep-from-getting-caught themes have the children in your care played? How do you think the children have benefited?

2. Kick the Can is a multi-tasking, fast-action escape-from-danger/keep-from-getting-caught game. Please review the rules for playing this game, and discuss its many socio-emotional and neuro-behavioral benefits.

3. What are some rhythmic dancing or chanting and movement games you played as a child or that you teach children now? Name several neuro-behavioral and socio-emotional benefits of these games.

4. What are some problems with cause–effect thinking that you have noticed with children?

5. Try actually playing a game of Charades, I Spy, or Hot/Cold with the people in your group if you are studying this chapter as a class. Experience how these indoor physical-movement parlor games can exercise the thinking part of your brain and influence your mood. What socio-emotional and self-confidence perks did you experience when you played one or more of these games?

6. Do you recall any creative play themes you played as a child that helped to reinforce the hero in you? Do you recall saving the day in play and making the way safe for others? What do you remember and how did that type of play help you become the put-the-well-being-of-others-first kind of person you are today?

Chapter 8

Where Do We Go from Here?

Where we are

A baby-boomer recently told me, "Parents play with their children? When I was a kid parents didn't play with their children—other kids played with their children."

"Truly," I responded. "But back when you and I were kids, post-World War II neighborhoods were teeming with hordes of children. There was always someone to play with. In those days, we were socialized by the 'pack', so to speak."

In previous generations, children who had problems at home or came from hurting places weren't alone. Although we didn't discuss our problems, we played with each other to help change our moods and have some sense of control in our worlds. Moving our bodies creatively and neuro-behaviorally helped bring us some sense of empowerment and peace. Our brains had better chances of overriding stressful emotions that emerged from within because the physical play positively impacted the neuro-behavioral systems which supported the smart part of our brains.

Now, for the most part, those socializing "packs" are gone and kids no longer have throngs of playing children to join. Families are smaller. Fewer children are around. Parents are busier. Supportive relatives aren't nearby. Today, children socialize by getting together for planned play dates or structured after-school and weekend activities. Otherwise, they usually occupy themselves with sedentary something on a screen.

Consequently, the physical games, play activities, and natural interdependent, cooperative, relational play experiences are becoming lost and their therapeutic value forgotten. Toys such as miniature figures that help develop hope and resilience through therapeutic play are now difficult to find. So are heavy, durable jump ropes or paddle balls that feed the sense of proprioception through the jarring of the joints.

Few children now practice cross-lateral (arms and/or legs crossing the midline of the body) physical movement that helps interhemispheric communication become more efficient. Those movements are just too hard now for too many.

Not many practice rhythmic chants, songs, and movement that help them become more consistently rhythmic as they move, speak, and interact with others.

Without rhythmic activities such as playing hopscotch or Jacks, or pogo-sticking and bike riding, children are neither developing rhythmic expression and coordination, nor becoming socialized human beings who are in sync with others.

One's internal rhythm should be set at birth because of an ideal, consistent, in utero maternal heartbeat rhythm of approximately 60–80 beats a minute. That rhythm should be practiced post-birth to calm minds and organize brains. Today we aren't practicing that rhythm enough. It's too easy to sit and practice attachment to electronic gaming and cell phones rather than to real, live human beings.

If someone has addiction in their DNA lineage, then the problem is compounded: the limbic system (emotional center) of the non-thinking brain needs and wants Dopamine, a brain chemical high. The feeling center of the brain can get this high from real connections to real people, and real physical play and movement, or it can go for the high that compulsive, toxic activities such as addictive computer gaming provide…and compulsive, addictive gaming can happen quickly. Chronically gaming kids remove themselves from real, live human interactions and seek Dopamine "hits" through electronics. Addicted to electronics, they can become detached from reality, socially unpleasant and inept, and physically and neuro-behaviorally impaired.

Add to that mixture a brain and a heart of a child hurt by in utero drugs, alcohol, stress, violence, neglect, and a post-utero early life of more of the same, and the reasoning and the "humanity" of the individual become more impaired and harder to find. As a species, we must not lose the capacity to connect to "real" others, to feel what others feel, to know where we end and another begins, to think on our feet, to control our impulses. If we do, then we lose the desire to give and we become takers.

We can turn this tide around before it's too late by returning to more consistent, interactive "real-world" activities and "real-world" relationships. So let's get *on our feet*, move our bodies, and play!

Ideas to help caregivers make physical play, non-virtual activities, and real relationships happen for the children in their care

TEACH CAREGIVERS HOW TO PLAY WITH THEIR HURTING CHILDREN

Most caregivers of traumatized, hurt children want to learn how to play with their kids in a therapeutic manner. Play is therapy that helps children's brains and bonds grow. In my private practice, I design neuro-behavioral and creative play themes for children that are based upon a child's specific needs. I then teach the caregivers how to carry out the therapeutic experiences at home. I call it a child-in-family approach.

I do not understand why the individual model of therapy (parent not in room) is still being practiced with hurting children. Parents have to know what to do when they get home. Home is where healing begins and ends. These children have to learn how to feel safe with and trust the good people who are raising them. Before children can form meaningful, connected relationships with those outside the home, they must learn how to be in healthy relationships with those at home who love them.

INFORM CAREGIVERS WHAT QUALITIES MAKE THE CHILD-IN-FAMILY APPROACH SUCCEED

Caregivers eager to help their hurting children would benefit from employing qualities that can best facilitate their children's healing.

Encourage them to:

- stay motivated to help their children become all they can be

- learn new knowledge and techniques to help their children

- make time to attend and participate in their children's therapy sessions

- review at home the information and handouts from the therapy sessions

- follow through on suggestions to continue the children's therapy at home

- work on themselves to remove child-induced psychological triggers

- resolve their own past abuses/losses that impede them from being their children's greatest helper.

SUPPORT CAREGIVERS WITH ADJUNCT NO-TECH PLAY AND RELATIONSHIP EXPERIENCES FOR THEIR HURTING CHILDREN BY CREATING SPECIALIZED, AFFORDABLE THERAPEUTIC PLAY CENTERS

Because neighborhoods no longer swarm with children seeking like-minded playmates who regularly engage in no-tech play, children need practice playing creatively, cooperatively, and interdependently with others. Affordable play centers can fill that need. They can provide children with adult-supervised activities that teach them to play neuro-behaviorally, creatively, and cooperatively interdependently with each other.

To help children's brains develop peacefulness where there was once anxiety or self-discipline where there once was chaos, play centers can also offer classes in therapeutic movement, such as hatha yoga or tai kwon do.

Each play center can be run by skilled workers who are trauma informed and sensitive to the brain regulation needs of children. While in malfunctioning fight–flight–freeze states, children can neither learn nor have fun. Trained workers would evaluate each child and create individualized play learning plans that target each child's neurobehavioral and social development needs. Recognizing and fulfilling what children need neuro-developmentally can make play meaningful. To be effective in habilitating and training the brain, play must be fun.

With an individualized plan for every participating child, skilled workers and caregivers may engage children in any number of the activities shared in this book to get them moving and interacting, and ultimately healing.

Where we can be

In therapy offices, at play centers, and especially in and around the home, children can heal from trauma. It takes committed skilled workers, willing, trained caregivers, and established therapeutic activities to help children benefit from the neuro-behavioral, creative, and cooperative skills that develop their brain, alter their attitude and bolster their bonds with others.

Through the techniques, activities, and games in this book, children's brains can be helped to evolve from fight–flight–freeze reactions to safe, socially comfortable, smart brain interactions. Children's brains can be helped to better organize and children can become better thinkers. And children's hearts can grow to not just absorb the Fruit of the Spirit but their actions can begin to demonstrate the fruits as well: active play, rhythm, repetition, community, and care work together. Children don't develop those life-changing, often life-saving skills sitting in front of a screen. They develop them in the "real world" while *on their feet!*

References

Bluestone, J. (2004) *The Fabric of Autism: Weaving the Threads into a Cogent Theory.* Seattle, WA: The Handle Institute.

Bluestone, J. (2003–6) Notes from Ms. Bluestone's trainings. Washington, Illinois, New Jersey, and Georgia.

Brown, K.L. (1956) "In the Heart of a Seed." In E.M. Bjoland (ed.) *The Child's World, Volume 1.* Chicago: The Child's World.

The Conjuring (2013) Dir: James Wan. Warner Brothers Pictures.

Gilden, L. and Marusich, L.R. (2009) "Contraction of time in attention-deficit hyperactivity disorder." *Neuropsychology 23*, 2, 265–269.

Greenfield, P.M. (2009) "Technology and informal education: What is taught, what is learned." *Science 323*, 5910, 69–71.

McClean, P.D. (1990) *The Triune Brain in Evolution: Role in Paleocerebral Functions.* New York: Springer.

The Miracle Worker (1962) Dir. Arthur Penn. United Artists.

Perry, B.D. (2006) "Applying Principles of Neurodevelopment to Clinical Work with Maltreated and Traumatized Children: The Neuro Sequential Model of Therapeutics." In N. Boyd Webb (ed.) *Working with Traumatized Youth in Child Welfare.* New York: Guilford Press.

Purvis, K.B., Cross, D.R., and Lyons-Sunshine, W. (2007) *The Connected Child: Bringing Hope and Healing to Your Adoptive Family.* New York: McGraw-Hill.

Purvis, K.B., Cross, D.R., Dansereau, D.F., and Parris, S.R. (2013) "Trust-based relational intervention (TBRI®): A systematic approach to complex developmental trauma." *Child and Youth Services 34*, 4, 1–28.

van der Kolk, B.A., Stone, L., West, J., Rhodes, A., *et al.* (2014) "Yoga as an adjunctive treatment for posttraumatic stress disorder: A randomized controlled trial." *Journal of Clinical Psychiatry 75*, 6, e559–e565.

About the Author

Beth Powell is a licensed clinical social worker, a certified Texas teacher, a yoga instructor, an adjunct college professor, and a psychotherapist who specializes in children who hurt, emotionally and neuro-behaviorally, because of their early chaotic experiences. She has helped birth and step parents, foster and adoptive parents, relative-kinship parents, educators, children's caseworkers and behavioral health professionals understand hurting children better and shown caregivers how to better help children recover from their early experiences. Beth particularly has taught the traditional children's games and creative play activities that she grew up playing in the late 1950s and 1960s to help caregivers meet the habilitative and developmental needs of the children in their care. She has stressed the relevance of rhythm, movement, and relationship to habilitate and develop young, growing brains, and those brains traumatized by neglect and abuse.

Powell is originally from Mississippi and currently lives in Conroe, Texas, part of the Greater Houston Metropolitan area, where she maintains her private psychotherapy, teaching, and training practice. She is available for workshops and lectures at your organization. Visit www.infamilyservices.com for more information.

Index